IMPROVISATION IN THE EXPRESSIVE AND PERFORMING ARTS

of related interest

New Developments in Expressive Arts Therapy
The Play of Poiesis
Edited by Ellen G. Levine and Stephen K. Levine
ISBN 978 1 78592 247 3
eISBN 978 1 78450 532 5

Poiesis
The Language of Psychology and the Speech of the Soul
Stephen K. Levine
ISBN 978 1 85302 488 7
ISBN (Large Print) 978 1 84985 061 2
eISBN 978 0 85700 074 3

Improvisation
Methods and Techniques for Music Therapy Clinicians, Educators, and Students
Tony Wigram
ISBN 978 1 78592 994 6
eISBN 978 1 84642 080 1

Presence and Process in Expressive Arts Work
At the Edge of Wonder
Herbert Eberhart and Sally Atkins
ISBN 978 1 84905 957 2
eISBN 978 0 85700 811 4

Anna Halprin
Dance – Process – Form
Gabriele Wittman, Ursula Schorn and Ronit Land
Forewords by Anna Halprin and Rudolf zur Lippe
ISBN 978 1 84905 472 0
eISBN 978 0 85700 851 0

Dramatherapy with Myth and Fairytale
The Golden Stories of Sesame
Jenny Pearson, Mary Smail and Pat Watts
Illustrated by Camilla Jessel
ISBN 978 1 84905 030 2
eISBN 978 0 85700 438 3

Using Expressive Arts to Work with Mind, Body and Emotions
Theory and Practice
Mark Pearson and Helen Wilson
ISBN 978 1 84905 031 9
eISBN 978 0 85700 189 4

IMPROVISATION IN THE EXPRESSIVE AND PERFORMING ARTS

The Relationship between Shaping and Letting-go

Beliz Demircioğlu

Foreword by Stephen K. Levine

Jessica Kingsley *Publishers*
London and Philadelphia

[permissions granted]

First published in 2019
by Jessica Kingsley Publishers
73 Collier Street
London N1 9BE, UK
and
400 Market Street, Suite 400
Philadelphia, PA 19106, USA

www.jkp.com

Library of Congress Cataloging in Publication Data
A CIP catalog record for this book is available from the Library of Congress

British Library Cataloguing in Publication Data
A CIP catalogue record for this book is available from the British Library

ISBN 978 1 78592 575 7
eISBN 978 1 78450 979 8

Printed and bound in Great Britain

To Ali Ekrem, Ali Emre, and their unique connection beyond time and space...

Contents

Foreword

Stephen K. Levine

In a museum in Istanbul, the dancer stands on a stone about one meter square, set several feet above the ground. She has very little room to move. Nevertheless, she dances, improvising movements in response to the limitations of the space and the surroundings in which she is performing. Her movements seem unpremeditated. There is no set form, but each variation seems to fit just right in the sequence. Suddenly water flows down from the ceiling above her, bathing her while she dances. Her movements change in response. The dance is beautiful.

This is what I remember from a performance that I saw several years ago by Beliz Demircioğlu, the author of this book. I had known her as a student in my doctoral classes in philosophy and research at the European Graduate School in Switzerland, where she seemed to be an attentive listener and a somewhat shy but insightful contributor to class discussions. However, I was unprepared for the effect that her performance had on me. I felt moved, touched by the effortless delicacy and power of the dance. It was as if the limitations she had set helped her open to a realm of new surprises, where unpredictable forms could emerge to create a whole.

I had the same experience while reading the dissertation on which this book is based. Nothing is predictable, yet each part seems to fit. Much to my surprise, the book itself has the same impact now each time I read and re-read it, as if the writing was itself a work of art that touches and inspires me and to which I can return over and over again. I say to myself, "Remember this!" as if my own thinking about *always* is exemplified in this work and, in fact, carried to new heights.

This book about the transformative power of art is itself transformative. It takes me into my own practice as a performing artist, as a therapist, and as a social change agent, reminding me to be open to whatever emerges, to never approach another person or group with a preconceived conception of who they are and what they are capable of; indeed, never to approach myself that way, but to always be open to new possibilities that will lead me to a future yet to be determined.

I believe the effect of the book rests on the transformative experience of the author herself. Beliz Demircioğlu opened herself up to a research process in which the outcome was unknown. Exploring the relationship between letting-go and shaping in movement improvisation with her research subjects—or better, collaborators—she participated in and responded to the experiences that they had in her studio, using in each case different art forms that fitted with what was emerging. This is research as *poiesis*, a process as much of letting-go as of shaping.

The standard form of research into human behavior usually involves having a well-formulated plan in advance and a clear method of discovery by which to proceed. The researcher stands aside and observes as objectively as possible, thus, in theory, avoiding prejudicing the outcome by her[1] own position. However, this is to treat the other person as an *It* in what Martin Buber calls an *I–It* relationship (1958). But other people are not objects that can be observed from afar. Rather, I am always in relationship to the other, even when this relationship is one of objectification. This relationship affects me, changes my being-in-the-world. I become either a "neutral" observer, one who is detached from what she sees. Or else I accept that the other who I see also sees me and affects me by his/her presence. In that case, I experience our relationship as a mixing, a being-together in which our separate outlines become blurred. I am myself no longer an *It* but rather a *Thou*, one whose being is always at risk in my encounter with otherness.

1 The pronoun 'she/her' has been used from Chapter 1 onwards for the sake of continuity. In the Turkish language there is no gender-neutral third person pronoun, so the author has used her gender for the third person throughout.

Beliz Demircioğlu put herself at risk in her research. She gave up knowing in advance what would happen and being in control of the process. Instead, she let herself go in response to what was emerging in relation to the other person, and found different means of creating that responded to the impact that the other had on her. The result was that not only were the people she worked with changed by the intensive improvisation processes in which they engaged, but she herself also underwent a transformation, one that affected not only her way of knowing but also her way of being, both in her art and in her life. This "effective response," as we call it, can be attested to in her ability to keep going while her beloved nephew was dying from cancer. The research process was literally life-saving for her.

Consequently, I believe the reader will *feel* the impact of her discoveries as well as *understand* them. In this research process, feeling and knowing are intertwined, as they are in the creative process of art-making itself. Creativity is neither a matter of pure inspiration, following an impulse blindly, nor is it something planned in advance according to a presupposed idea. That is to say, to use the Turkish words, it is neither *edilgen*, a state of passivity I surrender to completely, nor *etken*, an act that is deliberately planned. The very opposition active/passive severs the two phases of the creative act that are themselves always in relation to each other.

In letting-go to what is coming, I am always aware of my response without reflecting upon it from a distance. I shape what comes according to my aims and the material that is given to me. And in shaping, I am still receptive to what seems to "work" in the forms that emerge. As Beliz underlines in her text, creativity in art and life cannot be understood in terms of the dichotomy active/passive. Rather, the interplay of letting-go and shaping that are mixed in creative emergence is best described as a process of letting-be, one in which passive and active are never totally separated but mutually interpenetrate at different phases of discovery. The reader can see in the careful descriptions of her work with, not her "subjects," but what she calls her "Divers," those who allow themselves the risk of delving deeply into something that they cannot completely control or understand. The reader can only gain an insight into this process if he or she is willing to immerse him- or herself in these experiences. In other words, we all must become "Divers" to be able to read the book in the way it demands.

Why is it so difficult to do research in this way? For the same reason that it is difficult to make art or, for that matter, to live our daily lives this way. Human beings survive in vastly different environments by knowing and controlling what confronts them—or at least, so it seems. In reality, our knowledge is limited and our capacity to control the world is even more so. Life demands improvisation, as does art. But both living and art-making also require that we engage with what or who confronts us without knowing how we will react. And that means giving up the sense of safety that we can acquire in dominating the other by means of a preconceived plan of action. This is why we have "performance anxiety" when we wish to enter a creative process and why we continually resort to habit and preconceived ideas that interfere with our capacity to "dive" into the work. As Beliz states, we need to sensitize ourselves and let-go in order to create. If we can, we then enter a liminal state in which our resources are put into question. We may then become confused and frightened and look to another to help us overcome this state. This is why we search for experts and authorities that supposedly know the way. But an artist, a therapist, or any other change agent who leads us out of the wilderness betrays her vocation in doing so. What the leader must do instead is provide the support that will help us stay in chaos and will enable us to call upon our own resources, those that can lead us to take the next step, a step that had been covered over but can now be discerned.

I believe that that help can come through a reading of this book, a reading in which we let-go into the text and shape a response to it that is uniquely our own. In other words, the book, to be properly understood, demands a creative act on the part of the reader, one in which we fully engage ourselves with this work and let ourselves be changed in response. I wonder how many of us are willing to take this risk. All I can do is assure potential readers that the result may be well worth it, that surprises may come that can be life-sustaining and life-affirming. I wonder what my own response will be. Truly, I do not know in advance, but I hope I will be willing to take the chance. And, dear reader, I wonder, will you?

Acknowledgments

My most sincere thanks go to Stephen K. Levine for the superb mentorship that he has given to me. His guidance, support, and encouragement enabled me to approach the darkest moments as opportunities for growth. I am indebted to Paul Antze for his constructive criticism and support. Special thanks also go to my editor Paul Ben Itzak for his impeccable work throughout my writing process. I want to express my sincere gratitude to the Divers, who have shared their time, insights, experiences, and personal explorations with me. I thank my commissioning editor Jane Evans, production editor Emma Holak, editorial assistant Maddy Budd, and the faculty, administrators, and students of Istanbul Bilgi University Performing Arts Track for their support.

I would also like to thank: my parents Asuman and Ekrem Demircioğlu. They always lit my path through their wisdom, kindness, love, and constant support especially during dire times. My sister İpek Demircioğlu Teker. My words would not do justice. Maybe my dancing can potentially express the admiration, love, and gratitude I feel for her. My son Ali Emre for the endless inspiration and love. My nephews Ali Ekrem and Murat Atlas for the hope that they keep feeding me with. Aylin Kalem, Aylin Vartanyan, Ayşegül Altıntaş, Berrak Yedek, Maia Marinelli, and Ülkü Işık for supporting me spiritually throughout writing this book. Fuat Ören, Paolo J. Knill, Ellen Levine, Hagit Yakira, Ziya Azazi, Emel Alper, Candaş Baş, and the EGS Community for all the wonderful teachings. Ahmet Ayık for working tirelessly on the dragon illustration with me. Hatice & Cengiz Kırşan, Mesut Selami, Püren Savaş Gedikoğlu, Atilla Gedikoğlu, Burcu Y. Şeyben,

Burcu Halacoğlu, Figen Marangoz, Tuğba Ebren, Melis Ülken, Mine Dedekoca, Steven & Dilek Champs, Shara Claire, Maggie Pınar, Serkan Teker, Ceren & Utku Toprakseven, TZ women, Özlem Ersoy, Selay Yavaş Akbulut, Gulşan Hamidova, Şevki Anlayış, Gozel Alymova, Gül Saydam, Turgay Doğan, and CAGS class of 2011 for their friendship and support during this process. And finally, I would like to express my eternal gratitude to Tülin Ören for always helping me in finding my true north...

Preface

This book is an edited version of my doctoral dissertation supervised by Stephen Levine at the European Graduate School in Switzerland. It aims to illuminate the essence of the state arising from the interplay between letting-go and shaping in movement improvisation. The topic is explored through arts-based phenomenological research. From my point of view as the researcher, this book is also the *poiesis* (giving shape through surrendering to and listening to the process) that I held on to at a very dark phase of my life. In the course of the research and writing phases, my four-year-old nephew, Ali Ekrem Teker, was diagnosed with stage 4 of cancer (neuroblastoma). During the tough times of chemotherapy and stem cell transplantation I held on to the explorations and creation of this research. In this book, when I talk about the liminal, the threshold, I speak through an experience of living my life in that place. Life has taught me and my family to breathe, wake up, and laugh in the liminal. Just before I finalized the dissertation, my nephew passed on. At that point I fell into even darker places of the liminal where it was hard to breathe. My sister's strength gave me the courage and the burning desire to shape words into a work that could grow in others and hopefully honor my nephew in the exceptionally positive and creative way that he was.

I believe that this process is also a reflection of research as transformation. Exploring the process of movement improvisation and then molding the research into this book transformed not just my understanding of the topic, but also the way I handled the tough times I went through and myself as a whole. The therapeutic effect of the research phase infiltrated its way into our playing times with my nephew and my son. The final book became a product of *poiesis*. Instead of reminding us of the tough times we went through, it actually molded chaos and celebrated the wonderful existence of a unique person. Stephen Levine says, "the soul finds its form in art." I believe it also does in arts-based research.

CHAPTER 1

INTRODUCTION

Art enables us to forget ourselves by finding ourselves in the delight of experiencing the world about us in its varied qualities and forms.

John Dewey

This book attempts to delineate the conditions necessary for developing the relationship between the forces of what Expressive Arts (EXA) defines as "letting-go" and "shaping" in the context of movement improvisation and, more broadly, art-creating. While letting-go is more like a surrendering of control, shaping is an act of forming (these two terms are explained further in Chapter 5), and their relationship emerges, evolves, changes, and transforms itself through the different paths of an individual's creative and/or improvisational processes. Each individual also comprehends, senses, feels, interprets, explains, and visualizes this exploration in many different ways. From a phenomenological standpoint, I am interested in exploring the essentials of the relationship between these two forces, of letting-go and shaping.

I have been researching the interplay of letting-go and shaping as a dancer, teacher, and choreographer for 19 years now. For the past eight years my movement technique and improvisation classes for first-year performing arts students at Istanbul Bilgi University have provided me with an opportunity to develop this research. Most of the students I work with want to become actors when they graduate, but I also have students who want to become professional dancers, choreographers, performance artists, and directors. Most of them come from a beginner-level acting background.

They usually do not have much experience in free movement. In the first semester I lead them in what I call a "flow exercise." The students are asked to move freely from one end of the studio to the other. As they cross the floor repeatedly, I increase the difficulty by adding restrictions, such as keeping their hands on the floor or keeping their pelvis off the floor for the entire crossing, or leading the movement with a single body part. After a few weeks most of the students get used to doing this exercise, but for some it takes a long time to let-go and surrender to the moment. Around the middle of the semester I start explaining the concepts of letting-go and shaping, as well as the importance of creating an interplay between them. I emphasize the need to empower both forces in order to experience an inspirational creative state. Everything gets very complicated at this moment. While some of the students understand what I mean, others flounder. As they begin to shape, they start over-intellectualizing the process and cannot let-go. They lean towards functioning from their minds rather than from their whole bodies. Because creating an interplay between letting-go and shaping is something they have never experienced and that cannot be completely verbalized and understood by the mind exclusively, they get confused. The confusion only precipitates them into a spiral in which they think more and more. Others try to cope by going to the other extreme and completely surrendering to letting-go, which is both impossible and unproductive.

The students' aim should be to reach the state of "letting-be," in which letting-go and shaping work together in an interpenetrated manner instead of struggling against each other. It is not as if one becomes active and the other passive. For the purposes of this study, and to open up a more fluid operative mode for an understanding of the full range of the dynamic forces of both letting-go and shaping, and thus the grand potential for their collaboration, I have relied on the closest Turkish approximations of the English words "active" and "passive." "*Etken*," the Turkish word for active, is defined as "the power that has an effect, the one that has determining power"; "*edilgen*," the closest equivalent to the English "passive," means "the one who is affected by what is done" (Püsküllüoğlu 1994a, b). While someone who is "passive" in the English sense of the word will not necessarily be affected or changed "in their nature" by the actions of others or by the situations to which they are subjected, the definition of the Turkish word *edilgen* implies a state that needs its opposite *etken* and the possibility of some kind of movement or other action directed towards it in order to have meaning. The state of *edilgen* is an active, present awareness of the other. The chemistry and potential alchemy between these two states—how they can chemically change each other—as they maneuver and interact among the letting-go and shaping forces of an individual are analyzed in detail in this book.

In order to explore the *etken* and *edilgen* states of letting-go and shaping during their interplay, I interviewed my peers, examined my own process as an artist, and conducted dozens of one-to-one sessions with three recent performing arts graduates and four undergraduates. In the book I refer to this group of individuals as the "Divers." Their courage in diving deeply into this process and sharing it with me has been priceless. I had the privilege of accompanying them on their journeys while they went through them with all their resources, bumps in the road, dreams, and visualizations. I also had the chance to observe how they were often able to surpass their limits and barriers by accessing the full gamut of tools available to them in EXA.

THE DRAGON

Figure 1.1. Two-headed dragon illustration, created by Ahmet Ayık and myself

A few months after I began my research, I attended a contact improvisation session. In this movement practice where the participant explores listening and connection through points of contact, an image that symbolizes the relationship of the letting-go and shaping forces dawned on me: that of a two-headed dragon. Each head controlled one of the wings, while they shared control of the rest of the body. This image took the shape of a dragon because it best embodied the idea that both the letting-go and shaping forces within me were out of control. Each wanted to take charge of the improvisation. I realized that taming their natural instincts and helping them combine their strengths through being *etken* and *edilgen* was like creating an energy that flows like a radiance, in and around the dragon.

THE FIELD

When I started out on the journey of this book, I thought my research would be confined to the domain of the performing arts and, even more specifically, movement. But as I dived deeper into the research I realized that the art form under consideration was not as crucial to my research as I thought. My particular knowledge is in the area of contemporary dance. The Divers are students and junior professionals in acting, directing, contemporary dance, tango, and performance art. Even though the substance of this research has, thus, largely come from the performing arts, I believe that my findings can also be applied to the ability to improvise and adapt in many other areas, including life itself. I personally, for example, was immediately able to incorporate my findings on the dynamics of the relationship between letting-go and shaping into my writing and living processes.

I incorporated improvisational elements into my writing process for this book, not just in formulating and framing the content, but even in choosing the physical locations where I would sit down to write, listening to how each moment would inspire me to try different places. On some days I packed my bag, stepped out of the house, and randomly took different kinds of public transportation without having a preconceived idea of where I was going. Wherever the day took me, I did some of the thinking and writing there. This also became a method I incorporated in my mother and son days. We would go out and surrender ourselves completely to the moment to see where it would take us. I felt free and powerful by doing this. My son enjoyed it even more than I did. We were shaping the moment, and also letting it flow.

THE QUESTIONS

As I incorporated the ongoing results of my phenomenological research into my life, the questions posed by my study started to become clearer:

1. What are the critical steps in preparing for improvisation?
2. What composes the essence of the relationship between letting-go and shaping?
3. How do individuals describe the state of being that arises from exploring this relationship?
4. Can one become sensitized to the interplay of letting-go and shaping by using intermodal EXA methods?
5. Can EXA methods help remove the blocks to sensitivity and spur the desire for discovery?
6. How does traversing the state of letting-be transform the individual?

THE CONTENT

As I weeded through and attempted to sort dozens of hours of interviews, notes, drawings, photos of sculptures, and videos of improvisations, I realized the dimensions of the challenge of organizing all this information and presenting it in a coherent manner. In the end I decided to divide the book into the following:

In the "methodology" chapter, Chapter 2, I detail the arts-based research and EXA session architecture that I incorporated into the research of my theme.

In Chapter 3, I introduce the Divers, with portraits I created of each participant after the completion of our sessions. I also explain the process we went through with each Diver.

In Chapter 4, "The Passage," I explain the importance of preparation—the awakening of one's sensitivity and imagination—to a productive improvisation session, and explore different methods, regimes, and practices that can be integrated into the process of each individual.

In "The Journey" chapter, Chapter 5, I describe improvisation through the experiences of the Divers, myself, and other professionals, including noteworthy artists in dance and other fields. Experienced practitioners have created systems of exercises to structure improvisation, but this study does not cover the structuring of improvisation, itself worthy of its own book. Rather, it focuses on the inner processes that take place during all kinds of improvisation.

In Chapter 6, "The Essence," I set forth the necessary conditions for a relationship between letting-go and shaping.

In a post-face, in Chapter 7 I discuss the limited parameters of my enquiry and propose possible directions for future research

My "Conclusions" chapter, Chapter 8, is divided into three parts. In the first, I concentrate on understanding the relationship between letting-go and shaping as states of multiplicity, and portray the individual as an elastoplastic form that becomes transformed through letting-be. In the second part, I discuss the benefits of integrating EXA methods into the improvisation process. And in the third, I explain how the process of this book has affected me as a dancer and choreographer.

In Chapter 9, I gathered the responses of some of the Divers after the research was completed and some time had passed. Chapter 10 is for my last words.

My ultimate goal in this book is that the voices I have gathered—from students at the beginning of their careers and explorations, to established artists as varied as Salvador Dali and Twyla Tharp, to philosophers including Martin Buber and Maurice Merleau-Ponty, as well as accomplished scholars in the EXA field, and even my own voice as an artist and person as it evolved during this process—will leave the reader with both a macro and micro picture of the relationship of letting-go and shaping in the creative process and beyond.

CHAPTER 2

METHODOLOGY

If you think the Truth can be known from words,
If you think that the Sun and the Ocean
can pass through that tiny opening called the mouth.
O someone should start laughing!
Someone should start wildly laughing now!

Hafiz (quoted in Ladinsky 1996)

Improvisation is an intimate act. Suspending the rules of intellect-driven and preconceived creation leaves one refreshingly naked and vulnerable in a world of imagination, art, and endless possibilities. While it holds the potential to gracefully sweep away the sand and reach the traumatic material that one's unconscious has sequestered, it also offers great potential for discovery, sometimes through changing one's perspective and sometimes through enabling one to find something new.

In his article 'Expecting the unexpected: Improvisation as a method in art-based research,' Stephen Levine, a pioneer in Expressive Arts (EXA), proposes employing *l'imprévu*, that which cannot be anticipated, as a research method. He underlines a principle that I find to be critical for anyone involved in the performing arts: "We understand who we are through what we do and what we make. *Poiesis* implies shaping ourselves by shaping the world" (2013a, p.2). Therefore art is not just self-expression of the present state of the artist; it is a "search" that looks to her past, with its accumulation of many elements, including culture and experiences; her present; and her future—the unknown.

In order for improvisation to become this quest for discovery, one needs to dive into it with clear intentions. For example, while conducting research with the Divers for this book, I found myself many times trying to "prove" some of my ideas, and each time I had to transform my intentions and truly look at what was emerging. The same is true for improvisation in general: if one intends to go into it only to "express," not to "search," then a true potential gets lost. Since what I planned on researching was the relationship in improvisation itself, I had to use a research method into improvisation that would uncover this potential and keep the participants away from the mindset of proving an idea they already had before the improvisation began.

Arts-based research practices are used in different phases of qualitative research (data collection, analysis, interpretation, and representation) across the disciplines. According to Patricia Leavy (2009, p.3), "These emerging tools adapt the tenets of the creative arts in order to address social research questions in holistic and engaged ways in which theory and practice are interwined."

The EXA session model, with its carefully designed architecture and intermodal form, furnished a well-balanced structure, the freedom to engage in what is in some ways an intimate task—involving, as it does, not just abstract moving, but the subject's personal approach to multi-disciplinary creative improvisation—and, most importantly, the possibility of actually altering the subject's creative process going forward. While the talking segments that began and concluded our sessions tied our work to the life of the Diver, the theme-far decentering (when the shaping theme of the artistic process is not too closely related to the theme of the issues that came up in the talking segment) and aesthetic analysis created opportunities for the Diver to step away and really search. A movement improvisation was generally incorporated into the session either before or after the aesthetic analysis (see Table 2.1).

Table 2.1. The "architecture" of a session

Life of the Diver	Habitual world experience before the session
Opening of session	Connecting to the daily reality
Bridge	Guidance toward art-making or play

Art-making or play	Alternative world experience Decentering techniques Work-oriented Theme-far
Improvisation	With voice, movement, and/or spoken words
Aesthetic analysis	Recognizing the imaginary reality of both the art-making or play and the improvisation parts
Improvisation	With voice, movement, and/or spoken words
Aesthetic analysis	Recognizing the imaginary reality of the improvisation
Bridge or "harvesting"	Recollecting the effective reality
Closing of session	Connecting back to the opening of the session Homework
Life of the Diver	Habitual world experience is challenged

Note: This has an additional improvisation part added either before or after the aesthetic analysis. If the improvisation was practiced after the aesthetic analysis, a second aesthetic analysis was added to the structure.

Source: As structured in Knill, Levine, and Levine (2005)

The theme-far decentering was the key to all of the sessions. By carrying the Diver into alternative world experiences that could not be closely tied to her problematic matter, the range of play was increased. Once the Diver was able to get a taste of the surprising and unexpected experiences that happen in the theme-far decentering, she was more likely to be able to carry this attitude into the movement improvisation. Minimal talking during the transitions also helped this flow.

I chose to carry out arts-based phenomenological research because phenomenology examines the lived experience of individuals to reach an understanding of a deeper meaning of the human experience. Art in general and improvisation in particular give shape to the lived experience of the individual. Therefore in a way, artworks, in any medium, are phenomenological studies themselves. Imbued with this approach, movement has the opportunity to say what words cannot, words to say what drawings cannot, and drawings to say what movement cannot… Maintaining a phenomenological approach to the study of improvisation also provided a detailed and honest way of looking at individual experiences and exploring how their meaning is structured and construed. In *Researching Lived Experience*, Max van Manen points out that, "a description is a powerful one if it reawakens our basic experience of the phenomenon it describes, and in such a manner that we experience the more foundational grounds of the experience" (1990, p.122).

As I embraced this approach, the individuality of the Divers in the sessions was prioritized and empowered. I made a significant effort to make sure that they felt relaxed and comfortable to express themselves as their thoughts, feelings, and moods came to them. Self-censorship is the great enemy of phenomenological research, so in order to avoid any kind of censorship, creating an intimate world for myself and for the Divers in which true encounters could manifest themselves was a priority for me. These encounters ultimately did live up to what one of the founders of EXA, Paolo Knill (Knill *et al.* 2005), describes as meetings "between humans as peers, between humans and imagination, humans and art" (p.132). My understanding and sharing with the Divers of Martin Buber's philosophy on the Self and the Other (1958) played an important role in these encounters.

Buber emphasizes two different modes of existence: experience and relation. Experience belongs to the world of *I–It* and relation to *I–Thou*. Both modes are realized in how one positions oneself in relation to the Other because there is no stand-alone *I*. *I* is either the *I* of the *I–It* or *I–Thou*. For Buber, the *I* of the *I–It* "experiences" the world, but does not become a part of it. The Other, whether a person, a tree, or a dog, is an object. And the *I* can only perceive the Other in parts because it sets it at a distance. Since there is always a clear border, a separation between the Self and the Other, the *I* of the *I–It* can never grasp the Other in its entirety. She only observes the parts that are shown or visible to her. The word "experience" belongs to this kind of existence because "the man who experiences has no part in the world. For it is 'in him' and not between him and the world that the experience arises" (Buber 1958, p.5).

The *I* of the *I–Thou*, on the contrary, is formed through its *relation* to the Other, becoming itself through meeting the Other.

Buber explains that first the *I* opens itself to being a "whole being" in the present time. This "wholeness" includes the body in its biological and chemical composition as well as its intercourse with everything that surrounds it. By being in the state of a "whole being" one opens one's senses to both internal and external happenings. As pointed out by Stephen Levine for James Hillman, a psychologist whose thoughts carry great value for the foundation of EXA, "wholeness is the disease rather than the cure" (quoted in Knill *et al.* 2005, p.54). This statement is true if "wholeness" is conceived like the way post-modern thought sees it: a "pure" state to achieve. Levine goes on to say, "If we can give up trying to get ourselves together and instead find glory in what Shakespeare called our 'infinite variety,' then we can bring a quality of soul to our lives that will otherwise be lacking" (quoted in Knill *et al.* 2005, p.54). In my thinking I find this "infinite variety" the wholeness of the being. I define it as a state of acceptance of multiplicity and an interest to explore its variety. Wholeness is not flawlessness or uniformity. On the contrary, it is realized with the ability to draw a changeable frame around the uniqueness of one's own self and the ability to use everything that inhabits this frame as a resource (even the parts that seem paradoxical to each other). While the *I* of the *I–It* can never exist with the whole being, the *I* of the *I–Thou* can only exist with it. And then, as if a bridge is formed between them, both parties call each other *Thou* and walk towards each other. Their true encounter enables them to both exist in relation, so it is not like empathy in which one tries to look at the world through the eyes of the Other. The encounter enables the two to make contact and play at their borders, and their sum becomes larger than the two "others" that created it.

At the same time that it is impossible for an *I–Thou* to last through eternity—every *I* of the *I–Thou* transforms into the *I* of the *I–It* and has the potential to come to being *I–Thou* again. The world of the *I–It* is constructed around objects and therefore the life of it exists in the past. It is the state in which we spend the majority of our time and organize our lives. The *I–Thou* kind of existence, on the other hand, is very rare. The encounters that happen through I–Thou live in the present because the moment is filled with the two that open themselves and become the *Thou*s of each other. They have stepped away from the things that they experience and use, in short, the life of the objects.

Buber's philosophy has been something that I have been thinking about in the context of my life and relations as well as in my stance as a teacher, witness, change agent, choreographer, and dancer. In the course of this research I also came to realize that the relationship between letting-go and shaping has a lot to gain from this outlook. I will explain this in more detail in Chapter 5, "The Journey." For my sessions with the Divers I tried to be completely in the present and approach each one as a *Thou*. This was not a very easy process. According to Buber, as soon as the relation becomes permeated with "a means," the *Thou* is transformed into an *It*. My life has been and is totally immersed in this book. I think about it in everything I see, hear, or feel, but I also knew that I had to be able to step away from the main focus of the research a little in order to be fully with the Divers in the moment. I had to let things emerge even if they digressed from the subject as I envisioned it before starting the one-to-one session research phase. Deep down inside I also knew that this was the whole idea behind decentering, and that if I really opened myself to being a whole being with the Divers, I could possibly perceive different answers to my questions. So for the sessions, it was important for me to take away the "means" (concentrating on their experiences with letting-go and shaping, looking for the *etken* and *edilgen*), especially during the art-creating, improvisation parts. And in the talking segments, I slowly let these main topics emerge through the questions I asked.

Practicing the *I–Thou* kind of existence/relation with the Divers also by itself inspired the urge to give aesthetic responses. In EXA *aesthetic response* has two meanings. It is both the impact that the artistic work has on the client and an artistic elaboration of one's experience of the Other's artistic act or work. This second meaning refers to a unique way of giving a response that separates EXA from other therapy methods. In my work with the Divers, the need to give these kinds of responses was triggered by the I–Thou relationship rather than by a deliberate thought process. The aesthetic responses sometimes moved us to improvise together. These occurrences enabled me to live the encounter with the *Thou* in the lifeworld of the phenomenon of improvisation, and enriched my existence as a researcher and performer.

THE RESEARCHER'S ROLE

During the course of realizing the research for this book, my role shifted—sometimes even in the course of one session. I have been a change agent, a witness, and an active participant. These roles do not have completely separate tasks from each other; they frequently overlap. For example, a change agent in EXA terminology describes the person who holds the space by enabling the imagination and enlarging the play range for art to come forward. A change agent is fully involved in every part of the session, in order to see the direction that the creation wants to go and lead it towards that direction with minimal but effective interventions. A witness is a person who stays in the space where the art is being created with a complete openness to sense the emergence of the art, its effects on the creator and on herself. A witness does not intervene like a change agent. So a change agent is always a witness but a witness is not always a change agent. An active participant takes part in the artistic search. When I joined the Divers in their improvisations, I had entered their lifeworld as they had mine. I left my position as a change agent and became a Diver myself. One might say that a change agent also furnishes aesthetic responses, and during the process of creating those responses she is an active participant. I believe this to be true, but when I talk about being an active participant, it is about a larger amount of time, and rather than creating art as a response, it is a kind of art-making that places me in the same position as the Divers. Sometimes this involved improvising with them, and sometimes I was alone in this task.

SELECTION PROCESS

Throughout different phases of this research and writing I struggled with many challenges. My first challenge was the selection process of the Divers. I sent out an email with some questions to everyone who showed an interest in the project. These questions concentrated on asking the individuals about their creative processes, areas of interest, and their concerns and strengths in improvisation. I chose participants who had a sense of their letting-go and shaping forces during improvisation and who were aware of their need to work on improving them. I also tried to select people with different areas of interests, both professionally and personally. Based on these facts, the candidate pool was reduced to 15. Afterwards it became very hard for me to go further. I wanted to involve all 15 of the remaining candidates, but this was impossible, so only seven are included here.

I decided that because I was conducting research into letting-go and shaping, it would be important to involve this approach in all the different phases of my book. I stood in my small art studio at home, surrounded by books and different kinds of art materials. I randomly chose a book from the library and just at that moment decided that for each of the applicants I would first read their answers and then open a random page of this book and read that page. Afterwards, based on what I read, I would create a drawing or write a poem about that person in a fixed amount of time. The book I randomly chose was *A History of the World in 100 Objects* by Neil MacGregor (2010). The process was very interesting for me. It seemed as if nothing was random. It felt as if the object on that page was waiting for me to be read. The drawing I was going to make or the poem I would write about that person came into being through that random object. For Gülce Oral, for example, the object that I randomly chose from MacGregor's list was the "Flood Tablet," a clay writing tablet that pre-dates the epoch of Noah and his ark, about, as MacGregor puts it, "a man who is told by his god to build a boat and to load it with his family and animals, because a deluge is about to wipe humanity from the face of the Earth" (2010, p.84). I went ahead and created a drawing for her (see Figure 2.1). I did not initially tell Gülce about this part of the selection process. Once she was selected, in most of our subsequent sessions something about water came to the surface. In one of them Gülce said she felt like an underwater creature and like the whole dance studio seemed to be filled with water. At the end of that session I told her about the Flood Tablet and my drawing for her. She reminded me that years ago, when she had been my student, I had selected a song that reminded me of her by Zakir Hussein, and the song was called "Watergirl." I remembered. We smiled and shared a moment together, not knowing if this was a coincidence or if something had brought everything together.

Figure 2.1. Drawing created for Gülce Oral, in the selection process

After finalizing all the artworks for the selection process, I placed them in groups based on certain visual cues and made sure that there was at least one person from each group in the final selection.

SESSIONS

After the selection process, I held two-hour-long individual interviews with each Diver, that were recorded. One-to-one sessions lasting two to four hours were then carried out with each Diver; I conducted between four and ten sessions with each. In these sessions I tried my best to maintain an attitude without any presuppositions. With a phenomenological approach I tried to create a safe and sensitive environment in which the participants could explore, understand, and express in different mediums their paths towards finding their own rhythm between letting-go and shaping.

The sessions were shaped like an EXA therapy session, following this order:

- Filling-in: the Divers discussed their current state, and with a non-directive attitude, I tried to ask guiding questions to bring their thoughts and feelings about their creative processes, improvisations, and creating the interplay of letting-go and shaping in the moment to the surface.
- Decentering: this was explored with intermodal exercises; theme-far exercises were used to help the participants explore their imaginations deeply.
- Improvisation: a body-based improvisation that variously involved movement, sound, voice, and/or theater.
- Aesthetic analysis: looking, remembering and describing what has been done.
- Aesthetic response: an artistic response from me to their artistic act.
- Harvesting: bridging the imaginary reality of the artistic process with the issues that were discussed in the beginning of the session.

This was the major architecture that I tried to carry into the sessions, but with some of the Divers, I tried other methods. For example, with Hasan Canberk Karaçay, after holding several sessions guided by this architecture, I started becoming a witness to his rehearsal process. I still employed elements of EXA such as aesthetic response and decentering suggestions in these rehearsals, but I let him shape the main architecture while I alternately witnessed and participated in the creative process.

Another challenge was that all the texts that were created during this process, including in the artistic work and the talking sessions, were in Turkish. I translated all the material but sometimes, unfortunately, the artistic value and the impact of the words were, if not lost, at least diminished in translation.

As you might deduce from both my involved phenomenology and the multiple terrains of data harvesting—arts-based research, interviews, literary sources (with the added variable of chance), original artwork—once I sat down to write, I was faced with an intimidating amount of raw material. In formulating my observations and conclusions, it was thus impossible to confine myself to the questions as I had conceived them before actually starting the research. So much had evolved, including my approach. But to paraphrase Maurice Merleau-Ponty (1962), I realized that even though I felt lost, I was on the right path. "When phenomenology is true to its intent," Merleau-Ponty writes, "it never knows where it is going" (quoted in Fraleigh 1998, p.135). I was meant to change as an improviser during this process. In my initial proposal for this book I wrote:

> When I close my eyes and think of what the essence of this book is, the same visual image visits me. Someone is walking down a dirt path. It is almost dark but not yet, or maybe the sun is about to rise. This person could be a human being but it looks as if she is also a two-legged turtle. She carries her shell on her back. I don't know if she is carrying her home or just a hard shell to protect her body or a hard shell that also functions like a barrier. It surrounds her body. She and the shell are currently one body. She is walking. Slowly, with a stick in her hand. The path is dark. I don't see it. The forest that surrounds her is blue. Fantastic shades of blue, unknown and wild. Even the ferns, trees, and leaves... I don't know if I am that traveler or if this is my path towards realizing this book. Or maybe this is how I see the process of the Divers discovering, finding their own relationship of shaping and letting-go during their artistic explorations.

As I sat down to start writing the book, I realized that the two-legged turtle going through the path was actually me. Not just as a change agent/witness activating, observing, and deciphering the process of these Divers, but as a Diver myself. From that point on the image of the turtle that came to me in dreams and sometimes daydreams changed. She was still in a blue dark forest but the sides of her path were covered with trays of pastries and fruits. Even though the forest was dark, these trays were being lit from above, as if by a spotlight whose source was not seen.

CHAPTER 3

THE DIVERS

HASAN CANBERK KARAÇAY

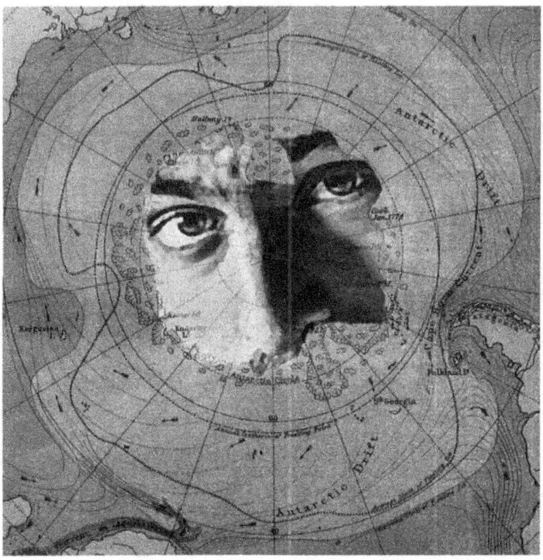

Figure 3.1. My portrait of Hasan Canberk Karaçay, created following our sessions. *Original photography taken by Merve Bozcu*

Canberk was in his junior year in the Performing Arts Department of Istanbul Bilgi University when we conducted our sessions. At the same time he was pursuing his studies, he was also performing professionally with two theater companies.

In his answers during the selection process for the Divers he said that he practiced movement improvisation three times per week. Apart from movement and theater he was interested in writing, reading, soccer, computer games, drawing, video art, and photography. He reported that physical limits and mental blocks were preventing him from expanding his movement vocabulary. He said that even though he believed he had been able to discover new movement, he got tired of always moving just to search for the "new." He shared that after continually getting stuck in this mode, even though he did not get physically fatigued, he got mentally tired and his working time became less and less efficient.

Canberk also said that he felt that he judged his points of departures too much, and that if he could find a way to stick to these points of inspiration during improvisation and develop them, then he could also potentially carry this attitude to his life outside of the studio.

After I read Canberk's answers to my selection questions, I randomly opened a page of the book *A History of the World in 100 Objects* (MacGregor 2010). The image of the Shiva and Parvati sculpture appeared in front of me. It was a black sculpture of Shiva himself in the middle, surrounded by tiny different figures. After I read about it, I wrote the lines in Figure 3.2.

Once I selected Canberk as one of the Divers, we conducted a two-hour interview. At the end of the interview I told him that we could also construct our sessions around the creation of a performance piece and asked him to come to our next session with project ideas. I hoped that by witnessing and in some cases shaping his creative process through different exercises, I could also better observe his concerns about mental and physical blocks during improvisation. He brought in four ideas and chose to focus on one that evolved around the story of a journey. The main theme concentrated on the journey of his ancestors from the Caucasus to Anatolia. We conducted our first session in a garden. I knew Canberk had well-developed vocal and movement improvisation techniques, but I wanted to work in other mediums in order to sensitize him in an alternate way, and hopefully bring the possible reasons for his mental blocks to the surface during movement improvisation. I supplied him with some materials to create a sculpture, and asked him to sing some traditional Caucasus songs as he was constructing his piece.

It approached from the back.
It touched just a point below your shoulder blade.
You didn't know what that point would reveal in you.
You couldn't even imagine.
maybe hundreds had touched that point.
But that moment, unexpected.
It approached you from the back at a moment where you had let go and only
touched that point.
Those that cannot be expressed through words flowed through your body.
It was as if suddenly a sac was opened below your bone, deep under your skin.
One could only stand and watch.
The one that approached was not talking through the language of words.
One could only just be with it.
To be, without a past or future.

Figure 3.2. Reflection after reading Canberk's answers and information on the randomly selected Shiva and Parvati sculpture

Later, in the aesthetic analysis part of the session, he shared some moments of doubt that appeared repeatedly during the working sessions as follows: "At moments like these, as I am creating something, an image or a shape comes to my mind and I immediately start doubting it. I ask myself if I have seen that image somewhere else. Now I feel as if I have to let these doubts go." This tendency towards doubting the image along with the tendency towards constant unnecessary filtering was a habitual concern that emerged. As we worked through the intermodal exercises, Canberk explained that at some points he realized that he stopped himself from making the desired decision and rather, made the choice that he believed he was required to make. For example, in one of the sessions I chose words from his automatic writing and asked him to tell me a story with those words. But I did not give him all the words at once. I whispered the words intermittently as he developed the story. Afterwards, while we were doing the aesthetic analysis, he confessed that as I whispered the words "rain" and "tulle" (fabric), the first thing that came to his mind was a drop gliding down the tulle, but he did not include this image in the story he was telling because he felt that the story should be mysterious. The realization of the belief that he had to make his work "mysterious," even at the moment of improvisation, and the understanding that he was constantly filtering ideas just to serve this belief, was an important step for our work together. As we progressed, I incorporated inter-modal exercises into movement improvisations. Canberk shared that "Looking at myself through other [created] physical materials opened a new and different space for me."

Canberk decided that the piece he wanted to create was to be a duet, and invited Gökdağ Yalçın, another Diver, to work with him. Rather than organizing the structure of a session, from that point on I tried to observe Canberk as he was planning his rehearsals. I intervened at some points and made recommendations. We also took a break after the rehearsals to discuss the process. Many of the topics I discuss later, in Chapters 5 and 6, "The Journey" and "The Essence," were brought up in these periods. Based on his background and interest in vocal improvisation, Canberk constructed a well-developed *Passage* (see Chapter 4) as a preparation. In my opinion the movement improvisation itself was more problematic than the preparation because the rules were not as clear as they were for the vocal improvisation. At this point in the creation, even though there was a clear storyline and the piece was divided into sections concentrating on certain specific themes, choosing certain physical limits to focus the movement improvisation could have been highly beneficial. I provided Canberk with a long list of subthemes under the main themes of space, time, energy, form, and body manipulation. These limits were tools to help Canberk and Gökdağ communicate, research, and develop, blending harmoniously together.

Canberk also decided to do the piece as his undergraduate thesis project. He developed it further with his thesis advisor, Aylin Kalem, and graduated in 2017.

After our work was finalized, as I sat down to create a portrait of Canberk (see Figure 3.1 above), I remembered him telling me of a song that told the story of the journey of his ancestors. As they were coming from the Caucasus to Anatolia many had died and their bodies were left in the waters of the Black Sea. One mother just could not leave her baby in the water and kept singing her baby lullabies. Canberk had told me this story made him very sad when he was a child. As I look at my portrait of Canberk, I see some parts of his face at the center of the water and the black streaks are like energy lines spreading into the sea. It feels as if the lines are almost moving, and the dynamic changes are caused by Canberk himself.

CANSU KUL

Figure 3.3. My portrait of Cansu Kul, created following our sessions. *Original photography taken by Cansu Kul*

Cansu had just graduated from the Performing Arts Department of Istanbul Bilgi University when we conducted our sessions. She had trained in modern and jazz dance before entering university.

In her answers for the selection questions she recounted that dance was the area in which she used her creativity most actively. She also designed envelopes, which pushed her to think of new methods for triggering creativity. She was interested in dance not just as a performer, but also as a choreographer.

Cansu said that she believed her biggest problem in improvisation to be the fact that she could not always let-go when she wanted to. Because she had actually experienced this feeling of letting-go, she felt uncomfortable when she could not return to that state. She said that while improvising, she got stuck on certain movement qualities or movement vocabulary. She said she believed that this was a problem she also faced in her life outside of the studio.

After I read Cansu's answers to my selection questions, I randomly opened a page of the book *A History of the World in 100 Objects* (MacGregor 2010) and the image of the Akan drum made in West Africa appeared. I wrote the poem shown in Figure 3.4.

It is necessary to sanctify the drum
It is necessary to respect the animal that gave its once-alive skin to here
Silently, it is necessary to first feel the instrument.
To say hello.
To ask how it is doing each time.
In order for the new rhythm to come,
It is necessary to stop and look at it with the eyes of a stranger as if meeting it for the first time.
may rhythm speak through you and it,
may it make you one.
Through the two of you
may it produce a new 'one' each time...

Figure 3.4. Reflection after reading Cansu's answers and information on the randomly selected Akan drum

Following the selection phase, in the interview I conducted with Cansu she expressed that in the past year she had been able to devote time, energy, and the concentration to develop her creative process skills while she was choreographing her undergraduate thesis project. As we discussed her process, I realized she was looking at "shaping" as a negative aspect and thinking that only the moments of "letting-go" were the resourceful ones. In our sessions, in order to let her experience how "shaping" can also feel like being in the moment, I tried to create intermodal Expressive Arts (EXA) exercises that distanced her from simple movement improvisation. I was concerned that if I gave her only movement-based exercises she would revert to more familiar, habitual patterns. During the sessions I first tried to sensitize her through various writing, clay-making, and sculpting exercises. Then, as she transitioned into the movement improvisation part of our session, I provided some of the material she had created in the sensitization exercises and gave her some limits to build relationships with these materials. During our last session Cansu expressed the idea that through these explorations she came to the realization that "shaping" could be a resource. Due to a variety of reasons we were unable to do as many sessions with Cansu as we did with other Divers. If we were able to carry our work further, I believe that we could have concentrated on ways to integrate this understanding into solely movement-based improvisation as well.

As I look at my collage portrait of Cansu (see Figure 3.3 above), it reminds me of a personal theme that came up repeatedly in a few of her works. In the aesthetic analysis part of a session she pointed out that most of her pieces were made up from parts but became whole in a certain way. One was made of reassembled torn pieces of paper; another was a small piece of clay supporting a very big piece. Another was made of aluminum foil she had wrapped around her leg in an improvisation. It kept falling off but she kept wrapping it, again and again. She saw these as representations of a constant effort, an effort to make a whole from the pieces, even if they had been separated on purpose.

EYÜP EMRE UÇARAY

Figure 3.5. My portrait of Eyüp Emre Uçaray, following our sessions

Emre graduated from the Performing Arts Department of Istanbul Bilgi University in 2014. Even when he was continuing his studies in the department he was working as a theater director professionally and had his own theater company. Apart from being his teacher, I had already collaborated with Emre professionally on several projects. I did not put him through the selection process but chose him automatically as one of the Divers. When we started our sessions together he was interested in finding a method for importing the creative process of rehearsals to the actual performance. He was interested in examining his process, as a director and as a performer, for understanding and communicating the experience of the liminal through the body. He said that taking risks and evolving along the path these risks take you was an important disposition for him. It was also crucial to him that the actors he worked with as a director assumed this stance with him in order to advance the work. Therefore my idea of *the Passage* (see Chapter 4) intersected with his interest in preparing both himself and the actors he worked with for *the Journey* (see Chapter 5), in which the liminal takes over.

As we started working together, Emre was having difficulties experiencing the liminal as a director, not just because of personal blocks, but also because of social expectations. The role of the director as the "all knowing" was a lot of pressure to take on. In the sessions, these concerns emerged mostly through movement improvisations. In the middle of different improvisation sessions, Emre started playing with two different representations of himself. They were conversing through movement, breath, or vocal improvisation. In the aesthetic analysis parts of the sessions he concentrated on how the more creative Emre (as he defined it) looked for balance and equality. With these improvisations he was able to be aware of, alert to, an aspect of himself by distancing from it. Duality was a concept both in himself and in the separation he was experiencing between himself and the actors. Half-way through the movement improvisations, in order to break these emerging divisive dualities, I tried to direct him into exercises that used three spatial divisions from the onset. At first he had difficulty with the setting. As we persevered, our conversations started to concentrate mostly on the themes of the third way and liminality. Throughout our process Emre realized the different dynamics he could personally experience in the relationship between letting-go and shaping, as well as the dynamics that needed to be resolved in the collaborative encounter between the actor and the director.

In my portrait of Emre (see Figure 3.5 above), both faces are the same. They look in the same way at each other. One has a shirt made up of sky and the other has the sea instead. They are different, but in balance.

GÖKDAĞ YALÇIN

Figure 3.6. My portrait of Gökdağ Yalçın, following our sessions

Gökdağ was in his sophomore and junior years in the Performing Arts Department of Istanbul Bilgi University during the time we conducted our sessions. Apart from his academic studies he was a professional tango dancer and teacher. In his answers for the selection process he expressed that tango, aikido, table tennis, and movement improvisation were creative disciplines in which he was able to fully or partially discard old habits and discover new terrain. Music was such a major inspiration for him that he had difficulty moving without it. Gökdağ said he worried that his physical capacity was insufficient, and this feeling of doubt disrupted the flow of his movements in improvisation. He explained that instead of concentrating on the movement itself, he spent too much time thinking about how he was moving. With his mind distracted by this worry, he was losing his concentration. He did not just *hope* that resolving this concern would also improve his ability to concentrate outside the studio, he explained—"I believe it."

After I read Gökdağ's answers to my selection questions, I opened a random page of the book, *A History of the World in 100 Objects* (MacGregor 2010). The image and the story of the Olmec stone mask appeared. After I read about it, I made the automatic drawing in Figure 3.7.

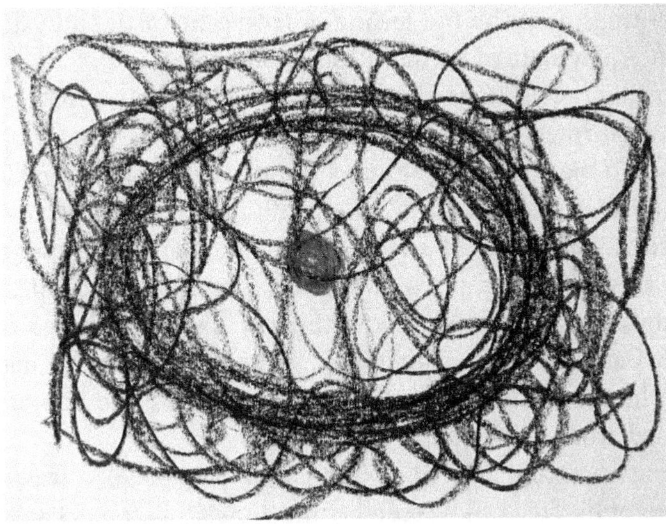

Figure 3.7. Reflection after reading Gökdağ's answers and information on the randomly selected Olmec stone mask (in his first interview after the selection process he expressed that he believed art to be the individual communicating with his own soul. This statement took me straight back to this drawing)

Gökdağ Yalçın and Gülce Oral were the first Divers I started working with. With Gökdağ, even though I wanted to incorporate artistic mediums like clay-making, drawing, and painting into our process, I immediately realized his resistance to experimenting in areas that he was not trained in. In our conversations I tried to explain the low-skill, high-sensitivity aspect of EXA, but my attempts were unsuccessful and this led to a modified approach. I knew he was a successful tango dancer/teacher and that in that genre he had experienced the relationship of shaping and letting-go on many different occasions. My intention was to help him find methods to carry that feeling of the relationship of letting-go and shaping into improvisation in general. I recommended that he keep a journal in which he could write down the ideas and thoughts that came to him around the topics that we were discussing. I was hoping this journal would provide written paths to merge his ongoing experiences in tango with our sessions, concentrating on contemporary movement improvisation. I believed that the writings in this journal describing what "being in the moment" felt like to him would be a personal resource that he could always go back to, in case his thoughts overcrowded his perspective.

His writings describe the feeling of letting-be in the purest sense (the interplay state of letting-go and shaping).

During the sessions I sometimes used interactive installations that transformed the visual image of his movements, and projected it live onto the wall of the studio. (These installations are explained in Chapter 4, "*The Passage*.") The addition of this, the live transformed video, provoked a sense of play in his improvisations. The themes of active/receptive, awareness, surrender, the third way, expectations, and doubts were primarily discussed, based on his improvisations. We concluded our sessions with a mind map, on which he drew a man jumping into the sea with the line of hope wrapped around his arm.

In my portrait of Gökdağ (see Figure 3.6 above), a watercolor portrait of his face can be seen behind a musical score. His passion for music and his expertise in transforming rhythms into movement in tango was something I highly appreciated. But in the context of contemporary dance improvisation, I felt that sometimes his tendency to transform music motifs into dance was blocking him from portraying his vast capability of creating movement for its own sake.

GÜLCE ORAL

Figure 3.8. My portrait of Gülce Oral, following our sessions

Gülce graduated from the Performing Arts Department of Istanbul Bilgi University in 2011. She has since carved out a successful career as a professional actress. She does not, however, hold such a restrictive definition of her work, preferring to think of herself not as an actress, but as someone who uses her body as an instrument. Apart from movement improvisations and theater rehearsals, she also sees her daily offstage activities as creative acts. She said that this perspective helps her break the routine of her life and transform the space she creates around her. She explained that the space she is referring to is not a physical area, but rather, a stance one takes in life.

In Gülce's responses during the selection process she stated that she has trouble letting-go during improvisation. Even though in the past she has easily been able to let-go and play with movement, in her current mindset she is obsessed with doing everything right. She said she believes that dissipating this block to letting-go would enable her to flow more smoothly in all aspects of her life.

After I read Gülce's answers to my questions, from my random selection of a page in the book *A History of the World in 100 Objects* (MacGregor 2010), the image of the Flood Tablet appeared. Afterwards I made the automatic drawing in Figure 3.9.

Figure 3.9. Reflection after reading Gülce's answers and information on the randomly selected Flood Tablet

Gülce's openness to try new things and excitement in playing with different artistic mediums helped us greatly in developing the work we did in the sessions. She was actively performing as we were working together, and this also provided us with an opportunity to see how the work we did was affecting her performance on stage.

I used intermodal exercises including installation-making, drawing, painting, writing, clay-making, and dancing (with and without interactive visuals) in our sessions. As we started our work, she was concerned mostly with her inability to let-go. As the sessions progressed she pointed out: "I realized what shaping is as I started explaining it in these sessions." The block that she was experiencing about letting-go was also caused by the restricted meaning she had attributed to shaping—she had previously viewed shaping as judging. I used the architecture of the EXA session for her to reveal to herself the cause of this perspective and to search for ways to transform it. The liminal (threshold) that she experienced in the course of our sessions also affected her daily life. She passed a dark path but her strength and will took her forward to a more fruitful place. Before I told her about my idea of the line of letting-go and shaping (explained in detail in Chapter 5, "The Journey"), a very similar idea emerged from one of her sculptures. The discussion sections of our sessions defined and empowered her experiences in the improvisation exercises.

While I had been her teacher in the past, I got to know Gülce even better as we worked professionally together. In my portrait of her (see Figure 3.8 above), I see that all the drawn lines are precise and mostly circular. Some parts are crowded but there are also empty places for new things to be drawn or to be regarded as spaces of tranquility, to balance the detailed nature of the other parts. The richness of her company comes from these details and the spaces she has to offer. The only other color standing out besides black and white is red.

ÖYKÜ OKTAY

Figure 3.10. My portrait of Öykü Oktay, following our sessions.
Original photography taken by Kevser Zeynep Meral

Öykü was in her sophomore year in the Performing Arts Department of Istanbul Bilgi University when we conducted our sessions. She was taking a year off to perform with a professional theater company in Germany. We conducted our sessions before her departure. In her answers to the selection questions she expressed an interest in how constantly playing with the text and movement evolved during rehearsals. Even if they did not move in a better direction and maybe they even took her to a dead end, the search and being constantly productive inspired her. She said she thought that when her rehearsal process got more intense, energy and time wise, the creativity spread into other areas of her life.

Öykü said that she had difficulty relaxing the constantly thinking part of her. She found great joy and satisfaction in improvisation exercises, which allowed her to find a dynamic balance between her shaping and letting-go forces. But finding a way to arrive at that unique rhythm of the two forces and accessing it whenever she wanted to was what concerned her most. She said she believed that resolving this difficulty would free her, both on stage and in life.

After I read Öykü's answers, the image I randomly selected from the book *A History of the World in 100 Objects* (MacGregor 2010) was the Tughra of Suleiman the Magnificent. Her answers and the Tughra inspired me to do the automatic drawing in Figure 3.11.

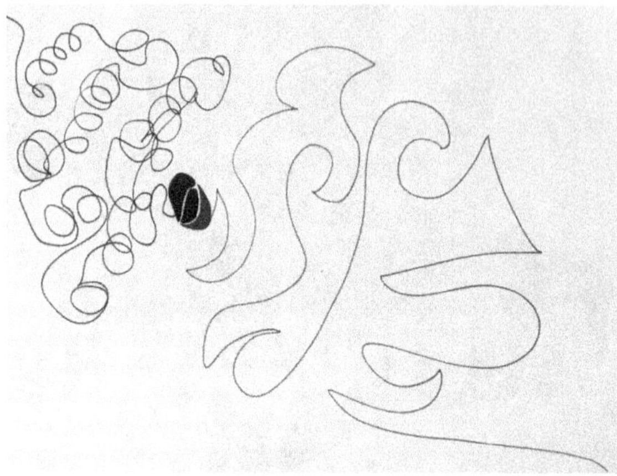

Figure 3.11. Reflection after reading Öykü's answers and information on the randomly selected Tughra of Suleiman the Magnificent

In the interview I conducted with Öykü following the selection phase she mentioned that as she strengthened her technical knowledge, her shaping force started taking over her improvisational process. She was able to balance her forces during her preparation processes (*Passage*) through music. She used humming as a way to understand the active nature of an *edilgen* (receptive) force.

As we continued our work with EXA exercises, a visual of a constant glasshouse around her came through. In the following sessions, I tried to incorporate exercises that produced three-dimensional materials before our movement improvisations. I thought that her movement space could be transformed in this way and maybe later she could comment on how the imagined glasshouse around her would transform as she moved in this space. "Creating these installations affected my sensitivity. I know what my body and voice can do but these materials triggered my curiosity. I usually tend to go to places that are familiar. Looking at a material that I do not know freed the movements of my body," she expressed. In one of the sessions, as we finished our work with the space she created, she mentioned her desire to see it from the outside. For our next session we invited one of her friends, Melda Tuzluca, to join us. Öykü set up the same spatial installation as she had created in the previous session. We started with Melda improvising in the space and Öykü watching her. We continued with a five-minute-long automatic writing exercise with both of them. Afterwards they chose eight words from their own writings and exchanged those words on paper with each other. Each one wrote a poem that included the other's eight words. When they finished, they stood up, read both their own automatic writing and the poem that was written by the other using the words selected from that text, and then started improvising in the space. In the aesthetic analysis we discussed how the space became transformed through this sharing of texts and improvisation. By the end of our sessions Öykü linked the receptivity of her letting-go and shaping forces to her spatial perception: "As the space grows, my forces become more receptive."

My portrait of Öykü (see Figure 3.10 above) is a double exposure of her and a tree. Her hair and dress seem like the branches and the leaves while the trunk plunges into her chest. As I was creating this portrait I had many technical difficulties and I kept asking myself why I was so passionate and stubborn about this tree. Now, as I look at it, I realize that it is because I imagine it to be a magical tree that spreads its roots down deep into the world and its branches up towards the sky, breaking any glass blockage that aims to keep it enclosed within.

SARVEN ÇANKAR

Figure 3.12. My portrait of Sarven Çankar, following our sessions. *Original photography taken by Alican Akcol*

Sarven was a junior in the Performing Arts Department of Istanbul Bilgi University when we conducted our sessions. He was also acting in a television series. Jewelry design, psychology, and metaphysics were other areas that interested him.

Sarven said that improvisation freed him. The difficulty he faced in this area concerned how to apply his learned thoughts, concepts, and ideas to improvisation without breaking the flow of experimentation. He felt that he separated his life outside of the studio with his improvisation practices, and was interested in finding ways to integrate each one with the other.

After I read Sarven's answers to my selection questions, as I randomly opened *A History of the World in 100 Objects* (MacGregor 2010), it felt like Hokusai's "The Great Wave" almost flew out of the pages. Afterwards, I made the automatic drawing/writing in Figures 3.13 and 3.14.

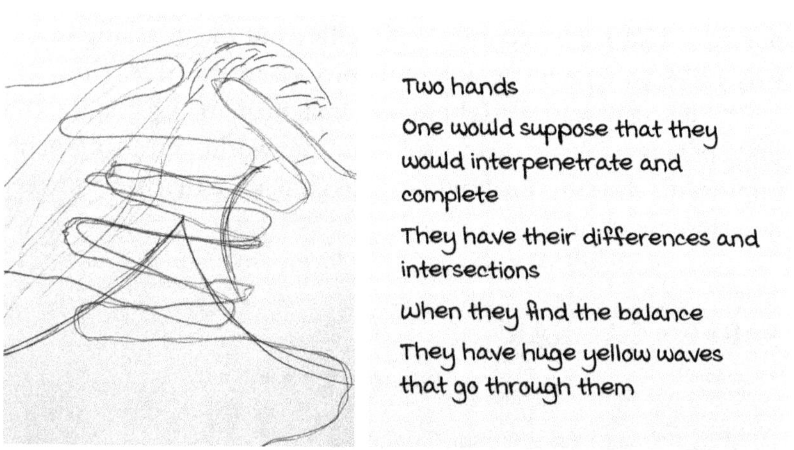

Figures 3.13 and 3.14. Reflections after reading Sarven's answers and information on the randomly selected Hokusai's "The Great Wave"

As we started our sessions with Sarven, his capability to achieve high sensitivity was very clear. In our first session he expressed the following: "As I start to really listen and receive all that surrounds me or the objects I focus on, my movement quality starts to change." In the following sessions, in order to assist him with his main concern of finding ways to create a dynamic balance between his shaping and letting-go forces, I embraced the low-skill, high-sensitivity approach. I directed him towards creating small installations from objects. He confirmed that doing these exercises helped him achieve the feeling that thinking did not separate him from being in the moment. In our conversations he pointed out what he had realized about the importance of this particular approach, and how thinking and shaping could be constructive resources. As we continued the sessions, I also observed that his hesitancy about being watched was transformed. He felt strong enough to make sincere and bold choices during improvisations rather than first thinking about how it would look. In later sessions our conversations started focusing on multiplicity and the possibility of productive chaos. Through his experience of letting-go and the shaping forces of improvisation he commented: "When one can be at a place where opposites can exist together, then one can give birth to order."

The aesthetic analysis parts of some sessions, in which he was able to see new ideas, connections, or meanings in the materials he created, underlined the importance of *poiesis*. Believing in the power of looking at the things one creates was a crucial theme of our sessions.

My portrait of Sarven (see Figure 3.12 above) reveals his face behind white paint with mist-like qualities. The thickness of the white emerges out of the paper, creating a texture. One side is more visible while the other is almost hidden, but the still, straight, and unclouded impression of his gaze still comes across.

CHAPTER 4

THE PASSAGE

In an interview with Guy Cools, choreographer/dancer Sidi Larbi Cherkaoui talks about allowing oneself to have a sudden transformation and "not being defined by what people see in you, or by what you see in yourself" (Cools 2012). The critical word here is *allowing*. The potential for transformation is there within and all around us, but turning one's body, mind, and soul into a flexible form that can take in, give out, process, and change is a complicated task. The pure simplicity of this mode de vie becomes complex in the context of our overwhelmingly multi-layered, multi-tasking, contemporary society. In the harvesting part of one of my sessions with Hasan Canberk Karaçay, he described this transformative process as follows:

> The state of the matter is important. The same material exposed to the same shock may show different reactions in different states of being. For instance, if the impact comes when the mud is soft, it changes the mud's form in a certain way. When the mud solidifies, it reacts differently to the same impact. It breaks into pieces and finds new form. The state one is in during an incident or experience is crucial.

The preparation, which I call "*The Passage*," before an improvisation or other creative process, is meant to take one into a highly sensitized state for approaching everything around one. It is an alchemy of different tasks, exercises, and rituals that change for each person. This *Passage* in some ways is similar to the "Rites of Passage" idea of ethnographer and folklorist Arnold van Gennep (1960), who analyzes the transitional stages of an individual from one status to another through different ceremonies in a given society. His observations enabled him to divide the "Rites of Passage" into three phases: separation, transition, and incorporation. *The Passage* I am researching with this book is much more based on the individual, and so, instead of concentrating on the changed status of an individual in society, it focuses on the transformed existence of the person from her own perspective.

Martin Buber's thoughts on constructing the Self through its relations to Others (1958) sets an important basis for the foundation of EXA and the research I am pursuing for this book. The pre-eminent theology philosopher identifies two different modes of existence, one concentrating on experience and the other on relation.

Buber explains that there is no such existence as just *I*, but rather, two states of existence: the *I* of the *I–It* and the *I* of the I–Thou. The *I–It* kind of existence, which is based on experience, considers the Other as an object. Therefore the *I* perceives and views the Other in parts, and can never grasp it in its entirety. *I–Thou*, on the other hand, establishes the world of relation. One of the most compelling conditions inherent in the *I–Thou* kind of existence is that the *I* becomes *I* through its relation to *Thou*. Through the relation *I* does not just experience the *Thou* but knows the *Thou* because of this meeting between the two whole beings. Each party has opened itself up to exist as a whole being. At this point the relation is mutual. They become a single whole.

The sensitivity difference between the *I–It* and *I–Thou* is the defining point for existence in *the Passage*. The *I* in the *I–It* erects a border between itself and others and creates a strong object–subject relationship, whereas the *I* in the *I–Thou* opens another dimension and really takes a step towards becoming a whole being. The boundary that separates *I* from the Other is destroyed for a certain amount of time and, as Buber says, "real living" starts to happen through meeting. This kind of *I* opens itself up to previously unimaginable possibilities.

When going through *the Passage*, one needs to try to connect with the world around one with this kind of heightened sensitivity.

The Passage's goal is to lead the person to a state in which she does not see or create art as a reflection of her mind but lets the form be molded into a work through her. Therefore a multi-dimensional state of being in which she can sense the range of forces in her and the others, objects, people, space, et cetera around her opens the individual to a richer kind of existence with endless opportunities.

With this book I am taking a closer look at, specifically, *the Passage* necessary for body-based improvisation in particular and the creative process in general to be fully engaged. Advancing oneself to a state of a whole being (acceptance of multiplicity and an interest to explore its variety) that constantly creates its own stance through its internal and external relations is crucial to improvising and creating art, even if you are not practicing contact improvisation or partnering. In order for the letting-go and shaping to have a productive relationship, the performer should first go through a *Passage* in which she can approach the range of forces in her own internal existence and become a "single whole." This way letting-go and shaping will not exist in an *I–It* relation but create their own *I–Thou* relation.

In this chapter while Part I concentrates on the sensitization, Part 2 examines the critical factors in the process of a *Passage* including intention, intermodal approach, breath, voice, spine, tranquility, and play.

PART I

Sensitization

Sensitization is a crucial part of EXA in all areas, including therapy, coaching, education, and conflict transformation. EXA is built on the idea of high sensitivity and low skill. The sensitivity aspect is important for everyone engaged in the process. In the case of this book the sensitivity research involved mostly the witness (myself) and the participating artists. But in some of the examples that came up in the interviews I conducted, points were also made about the high sensitivity of audiences. Tango dancer Aydın Kocamusaoğlu recalled a milonga—a social event for tango dancing like a tango dance party—in which the audience's heads and energy were directed towards him in a concentrated, unique way. He felt that even though there were others dancing around, it was as if those who were sitting and watching at the time had no choice but to look at him the whole time. A shared high sensitivity between the audience and the performer completes the spiraling rhythm of a state of being and feeds the artist's existence. One of the images that helps me visualize this state of being is the Indian time cycle (see Figure 4.1). In this perception of time, as the spiral grows, similar events take place but the circumstances change. As reflected in the nature of the shape, it builds on its past but also comes closer to or distances itself from certain periods. The dancer similarly builds movement with the connections she develops with herself, the objects around her, and the other parties with whom she interacts, also affected by their own sensitivities. As the spiral (or dancer) develops, it (or she) builds a history with the others and comes closer or distant to parts of this history from time to time.

In EXA, the word itself, "sensitivity," is used in a very literal way to mean increased multi-sensory awareness to one's environment. Artists of all kinds have used many different methods to elevate them to this level of high sensitivity. In a letter to Anna Maria Dalí, Salvador Dalí's sister, Federico García Lorca writes:

> ...I feel good. The house is big, surrounded by water and corpulent trees but this is not the truth. Here there is an incredible amount of historical melancholy which makes me remember that just, neutral atmosphere of your terrace, where Lidia sometimes lets out a stream of strong pepper so that everyone can be more aware of the visible grace of the air! (Dalí and Lorca 2004, p.98)

Figure 4.1. Indian time cycle
Source: US Geological Survey, Department of the Interior/USGS, spiral designed by Joseph Graham, William Newman, and John Stacy. Digital preparation by Will Stettner

Raising the sensitivity level creates space for "liminality" and for the senses to start feeding each other. "Liminality" is a term that was initially thought up by Arnold van Gennep during his research for *The Rites of Passage* (1960) and later developed by Victor Turner (1982). Based on Turner's perspective on the subject, Stephen Levine describes this liminality as "a time of confusion and powerlessness, as old identities and roles are abandoned and nothing has yet taken their place; but it is also a time of great creativity, in which one is free to invent new forms of meaning for oneself..." (quoted in Knill *et al.* 2005, p.43). So it is a time of great risk and also of freedom. Both the sensitivity of the *I–Thou* type of existence and the liminality open the person up for deep communication, internally and externally.

A few years ago, I used to imagine my *Passage* like that of the "Hüdai Yolu," described in a story that is passed on to generations orally. In this great Sufi tale, Dervish Aziz Mahmut Hüdâyî Hazrat needed to cross the Bosphorus from the Anatolian side of Istanbul to the European side to give a lecture. There were no bridges at the time and the only vehicle he could procure was a rowboat. A violent storm raged over the Bosphorus strait. Monstrous waves hit the rocks on the coast like they wanted to turn them into thin dust. Hz. Hüdâyî boarded the boat and started rowing towards Sarayburnu. Wherever he passed, a quiet and calm tunnel was formed in the storm and his disciples were able to follow in boats behind him and get to the destination point. This kind of a safe and isolated passage that felt like a tunnel was the imagery that came to me when I would get into the studio. Through time this exclusion from the outside world and the safety and calmness that this passage provided felt unnatural, inorganic. The chaos could feed me just as much as the still air, and I needed to be with the whole: the darks and lights, the storms and winds, the salty and sweet moments. The opposites and all that is in between them felt like the right environment in which to immerse myself for this search. I feel that I would not be able to be at this point if I had not experienced the safety of the calm and caring passages of my earlier years. The triggers that pushed me to take it further and to search for a much wider range appeared when I was ready.

The Passage is a place where I can check my connection to being the constant researcher. The high sensitivity of this kind of existence is an impossible and complex way to be all the time, so *the Passage* provides a path to go down in order to realize where one is and where one wants to be.

In an interview I conducted for this research, choreographer/dancer/teacher Berrak Yedek described her process of *the Passage* as follows:

> I don't really have a ritual I do all the time. What I do depends on what I am working on. But in general through music I try to create a kind of movement flow. In that flow somewhere I try to reach the state where I would like to be. I just try to listen

> to myself. And generally I try to do that in an empty space. I enter the studio alone. I think about where I am, where the flow is, the space, the things I have in my mind… By thinking of these things I let them emerge through me by themselves. I wait for them. And they usually emerge in the medium of movement through me. The quality of it is kind of always the same. Something very soft, flowing and sensitive. It feels as if I am holding something for the first time. It all starts from a point of relating to physical senses. The image I have for it is like this: I am a mass. All around me there are waves like sound waves, frequencies and many matters that are maybe unseen but they have an intensity. And through my passage I somehow transform my mass to become more transparent and make it go through those waves. And when those waves go through me I try to connect to them with my antennae and my own waves and flow together.

Creating an awakening that liberates and transforms one into a constant researcher is essential for a successful "journey" into improvisation and the creative process in general.

I sometimes imagine the whole process like a labyrinth. In the center of it all there is an amazing lake surrounded with different types of greens. There are also smaller lakes spread around different parts of the labyrinth. The things you are able to see and feel in the lake and the garden that surrounds it depend on which path you take to come to it. The plants, the colors, the air, the underwater world can change completely depending on your perspective, and your perspective depends on *the Passage* that leads you to that lake. Sometimes you do not even get to the center lake and end up in a small one somewhere else in the labyrinth. Each time you approach a lake you get excited because you do not know how it will seem to you that day. The trusting old feeling of that lake always being there grounds and comforts. One needs trust and some sense of safety to be able to move freely through the fields of creativity. On the other hand, while the possibility of not getting there on a given expedition makes one nervous, the lake's transforming, always changing form excites and brings newness to one's life each time.

The Passage is the preparation for *the Journey* but also a journey in itself. A great metaphor for this is provided by the "Hüsn-ü Aşk" ("Beauty and Love") magnum opus of Turkish Divan literature poet Şeyh Galip. On the surface it is the story of two lovers, a boy named Love and a girl named Beauty. They are born in the same village at the same time. As the years pass, they fall in love. The elders of the village tell Love that he will need to go to the land of Heart and bring Chemistry if he wants to be with Beauty. Love goes on this dangerous journey and takes Perseverance with him. Poetry, who appears as different characters during the journey, saves Love from many dangerous situations and guides him. After Love escapes from a witch, he crosses a sea of fire and meets the daughter of a Chinese emperor in a heavenly garden. This beautiful girl, named Seduction, gets Love drunk, takes him to the Castle of Representation and imprisons him. Seduction looks very much like Beauty, and Love believes that she actually is her. This Castle is the last obstacle that Love needs to overcome. It is difficult for him, but he burns the Castle down with the girl in it. He continues the journey but with wounds and an unbalanced nature. Poetry appears, this time as a doctor, and helps him get to the Castle of Beauty. The curtains open and as the lovers unite, Love realizes that actually from the beginning he and Beauty were one and the same. So the work's title, "Hüsn-ü Aşk," actually means "The Beauty of Love" rather than "Beauty and Love." The symbolic meaning here is the one Şeyh Galip aims to communicate, the journey towards being one, feeling that wholeness. In Sufism, this is the journey of a lifetime, an infinite goal.

The Passage is a more simplified version of this that aims to elevate the participant to a highly sensitized liminal level of oneness in which *poiesis* has a freer, broader, but at the same time deeper, space to draw upon. The art will not just become an exact reflection of the mind, like the way Stephen Nachmanovitch describes in his book *Free Play*, "…each dance, each drawing, each episode in life reflects our own mind back at us, complete with all its imperfections, exactly as it is" (1990, p.25). It will have the possibility of the "third" to speak through one.

Part II

The Process of the Passage

Creating a structure in your *Passage* that enables a changeable form rather than a strict ritualistic direction is important. This should be a structure that stands there as a core but enables the moments' treasures to traverse it. So in some ways it might be an eye opener to allow the letting-go and shaping melt even into this sensitization part. The focus of EXA is on an intermodal approach, and this is a crucial part in many different ways. Using multiple disciplines in one's *Passage* provides wider possibilities for play and imagination. It creates space for one to free oneself from constraining, repeating patterns. While the ritualistic part of *the Passage* focuses on diving into depth through repetition, the intermodal approach creates space in this depth.

Anyone who undertakes body-based improvisation work needs to create an individual *Passage* and be open to changing it as time flows. Some of the basic structure of my *Passage* existed for years, but during my sessions with the Divers, I have changed. I transformed my methods and fed myself with their findings and my findings that appeared through working with them. I am grateful for these changes and I know that there will be many more in the future, but there are also certain constant factors that one needs to pay attention to even if the methods change. The following are some of them.

INTENTION

The archer lifts his bamboo bow,
he draws it back slowly, relaxed,
he holds the arrow just long enough to allow the shot to
  mature,
and a perfect balance occurs:
with heightened awareness the archer lets go and opens up,
becoming one with the bow, the arrow, and the target.
The impact is heard but the shot continues beyond.

> Without aiming, the archer aimed at himself.
> Without looking to reach the target, the archer has reached himself.
>
> *(Jean-Pierre Poggi/Kyudo Québec)*

The Japanese martial art of archery Kyūdō focuses on getting the kyudojin (practitioner) into a state of shin-zen-bi, or "truth-goodness-beauty" (Kyudo Québec[1]). This is a state of wholeness, a mindless mindfulness. The kyudojin aims to become one with the bow, the arrow, and the target (Herrigel 1953). Through different disciplines and methods, *the Passage* of each person aims to bring them into this kind of sensitivity, in which the borders evaporate into thin air.

In my personal experience, as I enter the studio, the first thing I have to decide on is my intention regarding the connection of my outside life and studio life. Will I take the things that I am going through in my life directly into the studio and work with them, or will I steer towards a more indirect route, hanging my life like a coat in the corner of the studio and letting these things find their way into my work if they want to? Both the theme-near method (in which thematic aspects of the issue that is presented by the person are used in the structure of the decentering excercises) and the theme-far method (in which the shaping theme does not suggest a close connection to the issue that was raised in the talking segment) concentrate on this choice. Both approaches work as long as the intention is decided upon. Depending on what comes up in the studio as I improvise, this intention can also change, and I need to be flexible enough to realize that something is coming through and leading me in a way that will change that intention. As long as I am aware of it and accept the change, the flow of the improvisation continues. The flow can also still continue if I am aware of the things that are coming up in order for me to change my intention but reject this change and look for an alternative path with physicality, music, space, or something else. This part of my *Passage* is always the same; no matter what I am working on or what kind of approach I have towards that work, the "deciding on the intention" part never changes.

1 See www.kyudoquebec.org

INTERMODAL APPROACH

When I am developing a specific work and I want my improvisations to feed or open new perspectives for that work, after I set my intention, I either read something that I bring into the studio or do an automatic writing or automatic drawing session. The material I bring in to read is usually not directly related to my studio work but something that touches me in a way, even if I am unable to find its connection to the theme of my work at the time. Automatic writing or drawing is the commonly known exercise of writing or drawing without stopping for a fixed period of time and without any specific intention.

Whether I am working with an individual or a group, these exercises vary. One of the variations I employ that is effective is to make two people write for a specified amount of time and then select a number of words from their own compositions. Next they exchange the papers, with each creating a new piece of writing, usually a poem, from the words highlighted by the other. They are only given the selected words and not the entire piece of writing at this point. Here is an example that a dance couple created while I was working with them. They were just starting to work together so there was not much history or an underlying idea about the project. They were asked to write without thinking or stopping, in a limited amount of time.

An initial text by Partner #1 (with the selected words underlined), Derya Ömeroğlu read:

> (translated from Turkish)
>
> Did you already know that you wouldn't remember, is that why you stopped in front of the door? You stopped. I stopped. It didn't bark in between. You had candy in your pocket. <u>Didn't give it</u>. You didn't say. You ran around the things I haven't asked. A fountain in the middle, a few roses around it planted in the <u>ground</u>. A place that seems kitsch. A garden, a courtyard. You ran four rounds. I thought you wouldn't stop. I wasn't in me. I looked at me through you. <u>Frozen</u>, still, as if the life inside was taken out. A <u>woman</u> who is standing on the balcony of the second floor. Silent. No facial expression. The fountain started working. The cat ran away. You finished your rounds and left. The dog didn't bark. I didn't look from my self again. I <u>left</u> with you.

The second poem, created by Hüseyin Dağcı using the words selected by Derya from her full text, read:

> Was looking at the mirror
> I wanted a lot, you didn't give
> I wish you could erase the past
> I gave a lot, you didn't want
> Maybe here and now
> Wish you would never say I wish
> Did you ever
> Or
> Did you ever tear a frozen window and leave?
> Or I
> Have I ever seen a woman
> Have I ever buried her in the ground?

After they finished writing the poems they had created from the other's selected words, they shared their complete texts and then moved on to a contact improvisation.

Afterwards we had a talking session about the improvisation. Both dancers expressed that writing and re-processing the text transformed their perception of their bodily relationship, and then moving together transformed their understanding of the meaning of the text. Derya, who wrote the first free writing composition cited above, shared that when she read the last sentence of the poem that her partner constructed from the selected words she was very saddened and affected by it, and her improvisation started with that feeling but then, as she and Hüseyin dug deeper into dancing, she was not thinking about that anymore. While they were dancing there came a moment during which she had a strong feeling of being buried but she was being buried under water rather than in the ground, and it was a wonderful feeling, she said. The frightening, breathless perception of the act was completely transformed into a new understanding in which she even felt it was possible to breathe under water.

Inter-disciplinary exercises have a way of elevating the sensitivity for movement and enriching its content. Figures 4.2 and 4.3 were drawn by me during two different *Passages* I have gone through. Looked at before I started moving, each of these images shaped me differently. The clearly created neat lines of Figure 4.2 directed me towards that kind of a movement quality while the air-like form of some parts of Figure 4.3 led me to more circular and waving movements. Also, in the improvisations that followed my drawing these pictures, I was able to break free from my patterns and explore new ways of moving.

Figure 4.2. A drawing I made before an improvisation session

Figure 4.3. A drawing I made before an improvisation session

BREATH

Our brain waves work on different frequencies and these strongly affect our state of mind. Beta (14–40Hz), Alpha (7.5–14Hz) and Theta (4–7.5Hz) are three of these frequencies.

Beta is the state of alertness and logic that can also transform into stress and anxiety. While it can be our normal waking consciousness state, it can also be the brainwave frequency of the more intensive survival mode. High frequencies of Beta help you stay alive and operate with increased physical and cognitive capacities in situations in which you normally would not be able to. Operating on this level for much longer than necessary is a major problem these days. The stress level that accompanies this brain wave frequency is very high and produces many side effects.

Alpha brainwaves take over during relaxation, a light meditation, or successful visualization. They are the ideal waves to balance life because while they support learning and concentration, they also enhance the imagination.

Theta is seen during REM sleep, peak experiences, deep meditation, and creative states. With these brainwaves one connects to deeper creativity levels and spirituality, but the images revealed during this state are often hard for an awakened mind to retrieve. The mind needs the support of Alpha brainwaves to create a bridge between the Beta and Theta states in order to experience and have access to the memory of the content produced while in the Theta state. The creation of this bridge through the Alpha brainwaves is similar to the connection that is made through aesthetic analysis in EXA.

During *the Passage*, moving brainwaves from the commonly and unnecessarily used, busy and stressful Beta to an Alpha state is important. Beta is meant to be used in high-risk moments in which the individual tries to stay alive. By staying in Beta for a long time we increase our stress level. Certain sensitivities that are highly beneficial for art-making are also lowered due to the high-anxiety mode. Therefore the next part of my ritual focuses on calming the individual and helping them listen to their physical self.

I start by taking a little time to "observe" my breath—not to control or change it, just to observe it and where I am at physically. As Metin Hara states (2014, p.66):

> If you think that the thing you take in is only oxygen,
>
> Then you have not woken up to your truth in 'love'.

I have noticed that in times of emotional crisis I tend to hold my breath and then catch myself in attempts to take a big breath in. The cycle of my breathing unconsciously changes depending on my emotions and thoughts. The relationship of my mind/emotions with my breathing is a reflexive one. They feed, change, and follow the rhythm of each other. It is interesting to note that in the English language the word "inspiration" means both "the inhalation of air into the lungs" and "something that moves someone to act, create, or feel an emotion" (Oxford Dictionary).

In his book *Invasion of Love: The Path*, Hara describes the difference between breath and inspiration like this: "While 'breath' is about supplying the necessary oxygen to the body through inhalation from the nose and exhalation from the mouth, 'inspiration' is the energy part of this action" (2014, p.65).

After observing my inspiration, I try to inhale and exhale from my nose. This kind of inspiration exercise is used in many different disciplines, including yoga. It is also called a Sufi inspiration. I sit comfortably, close my eyes, and try to elongate my exhalations. I aim for my exhalations to be twice as long as my inhalations. Time is actually very important in this exercise. Hara emphasizes that this exercise needs to be practiced for a minimum of 10 uninterrupted minutes because the brain only starts to react to the inspiration after 5 minutes. Unfortunately in my *Passages* I usually do not have enough time to allocate 10 minutes to this exercise, but even in less than 10 minutes I start to feel more connected inside and outside.

VOICE

According to Kubilay Tunçer (2007, p.14):

> My voice is the mystery of my inspiration.
>
> My breath is hidden in my voice.
>
> (Translated from the Turkish; "inspiration" here refers to breath.)

These lines from a poem by Kubilay Tunçer, created for a dance choreography by Beyhan Murphy and based on Şeyh Galib's "Hüsn-ü Aşk," keep turning in my head. In one of our sessions Gülce Oral explained her need to relate to her voice physically. She lamented that in daily life she felt like she was unconsciously cutting her physical connection to her voice and was relating to it only through her mind. It is probably impossible to completely sever this physical connection, but even just not realizing it fully and taking it for granted creates a feeling of disconnectedness.

The topic of voice also came up while I was working with Hasan Canberk Karaçay. The way he approached inspiration and sound in his *Passage* profoundly influenced me. As I have been involved in his work with others as both a witness and a participant, observing the way he has built his *Passage* through sound has greatly intrigued me.

After three one-to-one sessions, we decide to take the work further by focusing on Canberk's process for his undergraduate thesis project. He is working with Gökdağ Yalçın on a movement-based duet about a journey. As the rehearsal begins, first, there is a talking session. It is very similar to the opening of a session in EXA, establishing a connection to the participants' daily reality. The thoughts and experiences that can be carried into the project are also brought to the table. Afterwards, each participant warms up physically alone. When everyone feels ready, Canberk invites us to sit somewhere together. If it is just Canberk and Gökdağ, they sit face to face. If I am also participating, we make a triangle. There is almost no talking. Canberk starts creating vocal sounds and asks us to join him in repeating them. He is really talented at playing with different sounds and melodies from around the world. He is scrupulous about listening to and sensing the people around him, and holding us safely in this medium of vocalizing in which he knows we are not as capable and comfortable as he is. This safety enables us to shelve any shyness and to dive into the process.

By making the initiating part of the voice travel through the neck and the head, Canberk deeply sensitizes the body to internal movement. Then, through the process, he builds a connection of high sensitivity between this internal movement of sound and breath and the reflection of this movement in the outside world, taking in what comes from fellow participants and harmonizing with it.

SPINE

Either before or after concentrating on the breath (the order changes depending on one's physical needs on the given day) it is crucial to focus on the spine. Getting the body warm physically is critical since the performing arts feed extensively on the variety the body has to offer. If the muscles are warm, they are able to take one through experiences without physical obstructions breaking the flow, but the muscles by themselves are not enough. The spine needs to be activated and needs to find its connections. The most important part of my personal *Passage* is waking up the spine. This strongly determines where *the Passage* will take me because the transformations in *the Passage* are mostly created by the range my spine has opened up. I can take in, shape, and process information from my body memory in different ways depending on the physical confidence, strength, fluidity, curiosity, and inclination towards risk-taking of my spine. Relaxing, moving, and really awakening the spine allows my entire nervous system to become more aware and present.

TRANQUILITY

As a dancer, I always look for moments of tranquility in between different types of intensity. It is one of the hardest states to attain and, once you reach, to let-go of. Throughout *the Passage*, even if there is music and I am feeding myself with it, I also always notice the silences, the tranquil moments. There are many different definitions and interpretations of what ritual is, but if we prime the Oxford Dictionary definition, "A series of actions or type of behavior regularly and invariably followed by someone," then I would say that the unchanging part of my ritual is these tranquil moments. They exist in the pauses between the inhalation and exhalation and exhalation and inhalation. They exist while a moment of stillness occupies my whole body and while I am awakening my spine. It is not that I am completely still in these moments, but rather, that I'm inhabited by a sense of stillness and silence. In reality these pauses usually last no more than several seconds, but they are the ones that take the perception of time out of the equation. The awareness, the consciousness of time, disappears. It is like an outer space feeling, as if there is no gravity, no sound… These moments of tranquility are the magic elements of *the Passage*. They evoke an indescribable light, which changes how everything looks and feels. They are sacred. As Peyami Safa said (1924, p.86):

> …Silence (tranquility) is the mother of the words. And its child also silence (tranquility).

I cherish my periods of silence. I celebrate them. I remember the times in my life when they made me feel uncomfortable, not in charge, self-conscious, broken… Now, with age and experience, they nurture me if I just let them be—if I let myself just be "in" and "with" these moments. There are pauses spread everywhere in our lives. It is exhausting to listen to people who talk without them. Music sometimes makes its strongest impact when punctuated by silence, as does dance. Busy architecture makes less impact than architecture that incorporates empty space into its design.

Otto Friedrich Bollnow offers a similar observation about conversation:

> …When the conversation finally does sink into silence, it is no empty silence, but a fulfilled silence. The truth, not only of the insight that has been acquired, but the truth of life, the state of being in truth that has been achieved in the conversation, continues to make itself felt, indeed becomes deeper, in the course of this silence. (quoted in van Manen 1990, p.99)

PLAY

In his book *Play*, Stuart Brown (2010) talks about how through playing, we learn the mystery and excitement that can be found in simple things. This joyful feeling is directly related to our attitude.

Many people strive to retain an amateur spirit towards their profession, even if they have become an expert. The word "amateur" derives from the Latin word "amātor," which means "lover." When one really loves something and finds oneself in an *I–Thou* relation with it, this relation, Buber notes, "fills the heavens. This does not mean that nothing else exists; but that all else lives in its light" (1958, p.78). Finding this love is critical, and one of the channels for securing it is play. It is something that everyone has tasted at least once in their life, so a strong reference to it already exists.

For some of the sessions for this book I designed interactive installations to inspire the sense of play. These are big projections that use live image processing. As the participant stands in front of a fully projected wall, she sees herself in her real-life size, without any delays. Her image is changed depending on what kind of a design I have created. For one of the sessions I held with Gökdağ Yalçın, I created an installation in which his projection seemed more like a mixture of his body and light, expanding his movements between his starting point and ending point (see Figure 4.4). Gökdağ described the process like this:

> I felt like a child. Children discover. For them, the game they are playing is the most important thing in the world. The feeling of making something the most important thing in the world for that time in space is really beautiful. I think being in the moment is like that. There were times when I was moving with the interactive projection where I thought, how do I look from outside...? If the recording of me doing this is shown, what will the people who watch it think...? I wasn't just NOT in the moment, I was three years ahead. It was a very full feeling when I left these thoughts aside and just played. There were two kinds of play. One where I just let go and played with the visual and another where I set up a game and played with my movement within the rules of that game. Both were fun.

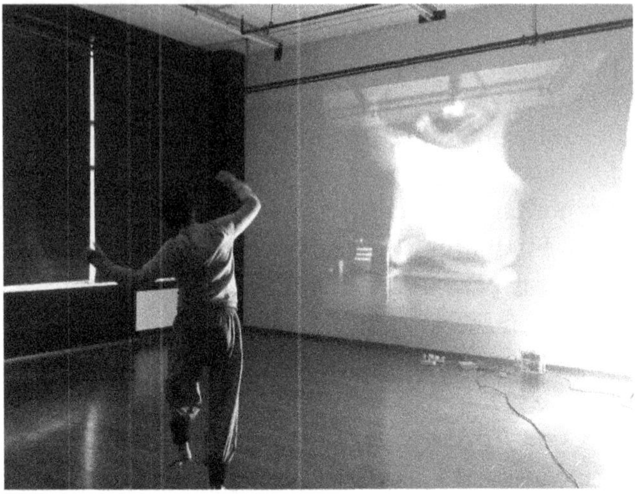

Figure 4.4. Gökdağ Yalçın improvising with the interactive projection

It was inspiring to watch the change in the movement quality over the course of Gökdağ's improvisation. He was able to break free from his movement patterns and discover new ways of moving. At the time it was not even important that he had a moment of realization about this aspect of the experience. There were three major goals that were being accomplished. First, he was able to be fully in the moment—maintaining a certain spontaneity—but at the same time able to integrate shaping into it by constructing a game. Second, his body was able to assimilate all these new ways of moving into its memory even if he did not consciously realize the mechanics of the new movements. Through the new movements his sensitivity was increased because the projection was changing the appearance of the forms he was creating based on his movement and his interaction with the space. Even when his image was distorted, he was realizing all the things that were happening in the middle of big movements, and started approaching the movement with a new, detailed sensitivity. Finally, his movement vocabulary was broadened. (Though this was true primarily in the context of the sensitization of this session, and might not necessarily carry over to his future work. We did not do a time-based study, which would have allowed us to look at the effects of this on his movement vocabulary in improvisation in general.) I was able to observe the differences in this session because Gökdağ had been a student of mine for some time, and also because he mentioned them at the closing of the session.

In another session, Gülce Oral took charge of the small camera that was on the floor, integrating it into her movements, controlling where the eye of the camera looked, and what the projection would reflect. She described her experience as follows:

> This time I did not separate the projection from myself. The whole space opened up and transformed with the image. It was like I was underwater. The whole room was water. At the session before when I first saw my image, I forgot that I was moving here. And then it was like I was not physically in the thing that I was doing… But in this session sometimes me, the camera, my shadow—it was all one. It felt like I was making peace with myself. And sometimes I saw the camera as a sea creature and I saw my reflection through the eyes of that creature.

There are many different ways to integrate the sense of play into *the Passage*, and interactivity is one of them. The unique opportunity it provides is that it enables an encounter with a slightly changed form of the self without a delay and therefore provides another space — the matrix of the projection—to break patterns and search.

CHAPTER 5

THE JOURNEY

Every angel is terrifying.

Rainer Maria Rilke

This chapter is itself an exploration into the improvisation journey, looking into its most critical aspects: body, poiesis, liminality, chaos, letting-go and shaping, the infinity line of letting-go and shaping, letting-be, etken and edilgen, art and life.

Part I

Body

The work of Maurice Merleau-Ponty is illuminating in examining the dynamics of improvisation. In his book *Phenomenology of Perception*, Merleau-Ponty (1962) challenges the Cartesian dualism of mind and body and develops an understanding of perception that concentrates on human beings as embodied subjects that perceive the world through their senses. The meanings we create do not appear as a result of disembodied consciousness, but rather, through our body's lived experience: "We are caught up in the world and we do not succeed in extricating ourselves from it in order to achieve consciousness of the world" (Merleau-Ponty 1962, p.5). Therefore our uniqueness in perceiving the world comes from our authentic bodily existence. Merleau-Ponty calls this existence "*the lived body*," and differentiates it from the objective body. Stephen Levine defines the objective body as "elements disconnected from one another, a mechanical system lacking the intentional experience of being-in-the-world" (Levine 2009, p.122).

In *The Man Who Mistook His Wife for a Hat*, neurologist Oliver Sacks (1985) shares the mind-altering stories of some of his patients. In the account to which the book owes its title, he writes about Dr P., a distinguished musician/teacher. Dr P. consults Sacks more after the urging of others in his entourage than out of any innate concern for himself. He explains that sometimes he does not recognize certain people when he sees them, but once they speak, he can identify them. He has a quirky sense of humor and laughs at himself as he explains that sometimes he even pats the heads of water hydrants or parking meters because he mistakes them for people. He reports that after carefully examining his eyes, his ophthalmologist refers him to a neurologist to get the visual part of his brain checked. After examining Dr P., Sacks diagnoses him with visual agnosia. So Dr P. can actually see everything, but because of damage in the visual part of his brain, his perception is affected. On the other hand, as a musician who has built his daily life around music, he is now capable of transforming the visual cues of movement into aural perceptions. For example, he might not be able to recognize a student sitting right in front of him, but if the student gets up and starts to move, Dr P. is capable of observing, "That's Karl, I know his movements, his body music" (Sacks 1985, p.21). The story of Dr P. underlines the importance of understanding the authenticity of the *lived body*. Merleau-Ponty argues that there is no one uniform definition of perception but only individual perceptions as they are lived in the world (quoted in Broadhurst 2007). And Dr P. shows us that even though the unity of the perceptual experience might be altered by a brain tumor, the body is still capable of interpreting the visual stimuli as sound without feeling disturbed or concentrating on the lacking component. His unique adjustment is tailored to maximize his strengths rather than diminished to cater to his weaknesses.

Merleau-Ponty goes on to say that it is the body that "gives significance not only to the natural object, but also to cultural objects like words" (1962, p.235). He details an experiment in which if a word like "hard" is shown to a subject for too short an amount of time for him to be able to read it, the subject feels a stiffness in his back and neck. These are subliminal stimuli that escape our conscious perception (Wikipedia 2016a). Images and audio can be used in this way. We all receive many kinds of subliminal stimuli, some intentionally sent to us—by advertisers, for example—some environmental. Received through different senses, these subliminal stimuli fall below our conscious radar but they do affect our bodies and our minds. The example given by Merleau-Ponty makes us realize three factors that are exceptionally critical for improvisation. First, it is through our bodies that we receive stimuli that are both below and above our conscious perception. So the body and mind get reunited. Second, our bodies and minds are subjected to much more stimuli than we imagine. And third, they are able to receive, process, and transform these stimuli into expression.

The power of the inter-disciplinary exercises in *the Passage* partially comes from this understanding that the body assigns significance to cultural objects like words or literal images. After *the Passage* these perceptions are already present in the body when the improviser starts. Improvisation empowers her to incorporate/transform them with movement and/or transform the movement with the perceptions, or ideas, of cultural objects like literary images or words. As we progress from *the Passage* into *the Journey*, it is important to realize that Merleau-Ponty's understanding of the *lived body*, as opposed to purely intellect-driven consciousness, informs the capacity to listen to and receive in various forms all that surrounds us. *The Journey* uses this capacity that has been empowered by *the Passage*.

Part II

Poiesis

In Expressive Arts (EXA), *poiesis* is the process through which the artist, using her own way of sensing and shaping, directs chaos into finding a shape. The artist sets forth to become the mediator for the particular creation to come together. She does not see herself as the "demiurge who creates *ex-nihilo*" (Levine, quoted in Knill *et al.* 2005, p.40). Surrendering is one of the keys here in two different forms. Surrendering for letting-go enables the artist to become more receptive; instead of just actualizing preconceived ideas about an artwork, she is able to experience the moment and be open to what will emerge. Surrendering for shaping clears the process from immediate self-judgment and doubt. Levine sees the process of *poiesis* as a "chaotic fragmentation that the artist must willingly undergo in order to shape a new form. In the light of the finished product what was there before makes perfect sense; however, before it arrived, all was obscure and unclear" (quoted in Knill *et al.* 2005, p.41).

Sometimes the process can be so chaotic that it may take even longer than anticipated for the finished product to make sense. I experienced this clearly in a performance piece I created in collaboration with Aylin Kalem, Güneş Çağlar, Selçuk Artut, and Ercan Cihandide called "The Knot Theory" (see Figure 5.1). It was a contemporary dance in which Artut captured live sounds and visuals on stage in real time, processed them, and projected them back on stage. When I began working on the piece in a three-week residency at L'animal a l'esquena (in Spain) with Aylin and Güneş, I only had a general idea of what I wanted to work on. We completely surrendered to the chaos together and shaped it into a 45-minute multi-media dance. Even though the whole process lasted for more than six months, it still seemed like the piece was obscure and unclear when I first performed it. On stage, I felt completely immersed in the world of this creation and it moved me, but when I looked at it from the outside, intellectually, I was unable to understand some of the choices I had made as a choreographer. It was clear that I would never have created something like this with a preconceived process, and this realization made me question the validity of the work. It was my ego, which believes it knows exactly who I am and who I will become, that felt uncomfortable with my signing my name to a work that it could not fully grasp. It took me several months to fully understand what the work was communicating to me. It felt like new aesthetic choices for my future were talking to me through this work and maturing me. If we had not surrendered ourselves to the chaos and moved into the threshold of living and shaping this chaos, the outcome would have been completely different. Most probably the work would not have taught me so much.

Figure 5.1. "The Knot Theory" residency at L'animal a l'esquena

Part III

Liminality

As mentioned in Chapter 4, the term "limin," Latin for "threshold," was developed by anthropologist Arnold van Gennep, whose *The Rites of Passage* (first published in 1908) analyzed the rituals that accompany an individual or group's path in transforming their social status. Van Gennep called the process the "Rites of Passage" and divided it into three parts: *separation*, *transition*, and *incorporation* (1960). The first part involves a detachment from the former self—both leaving the mother's womb to come into this world and cutting one's hair before joining the army are examples of *separation*. The *transition* stage, which van Gennep calls "limin," is a phase of flux. It is a period in which the attributes related to the previous social status are left behind and new ones are discovered. This phase is especially important for the study of improvisation. In the third and final stage, *incorporation*, the individual returns to society with her newly found social status. An example that clearly illustrates the three stages of van Gennep's theory is found in the ceremonies of the Brahmin. In Hinduism, the Brahmin are the highest of the four castes of Hindu society. A Brahmin belongs to his caste by birth but is considered to be born again after he undergoes a sacred ceremony. After he is born into this caste, he needs to learn to act like a Brahmin and later undergoes initiation ceremonies that symbolize his death in the old world and his birth in the new one. In these ceremonies he is given the power to devote himself to his occupational specialty. As van Gennep writes, "Within the sacred world which Brahmin inhabits from birth there are three compartments: a preliminal one lasting until the *upanayana* (the beginning of a relationship with a teacher), a liminal one (novitiate), and a postliminal one (priesthood)" (1960, p.105).

For the study of improvisation, the properties of the middle part, the limin, hold crucial value. We can even say that if *separation* involves leaving one's daily life and stepping into the studio, *transition* is the improvisation and *incorporation* entails returning to daily life with the treasures that are gained in the liminal state. Victor Turner, a cultural anthropologist who studied liminality in depth, defines it as an ambiguous state that for many may be more the "acme of insecurity, the breakthrough of chaos into cosmos, of disorder into order, than the milieu of creative inter-human or transhuman satisfactions and achievements" (1982, p.46). In her article "Exploring the work of Victor Turner: Liminality and its later implications," Edith Turner, an anthropologist and also Victor Turner's wife, recalls a period of living this in-between-ness from their own lives:

> Our house was beside the Bourne, a stream that joined land to sea; our daughter Rene was a teenager, neither a child nor an adult; and both Turner and I were in the middle of a complex change in our entire anthropological philosophy. Worse, there occurred John Kennedy's assassination. This was threshold living at every moment. (2008, p.35)

Liminality exists as a temporary state. It is a transition between two stable states. One might say that the preceding and subsequent states are like Buber's *I–It* kind of existence (discussed in Chapter 2), in which the individual relates to everything around her with an object–subject perspective. She knows and defines herself clearly and apart from others. Life mostly happens here but the flair, the enrichment, comes from the temporary part: the liminal. As with the *I–Thou* relationship, in the liminal stage one opens oneself up to all the possibilities. It is like being a teenager who walks into the woods in order to live an adventure. In this journey she discovers her own name through her actions and experiences rather than just accepting what she has inherited. She approaches herself as well as the wild and unknown with a curious and open mind. This outlook, directed both towards oneself and one's surroundings, is critical for the liminal state because only then can a blurring, merging, and transformation of preconceived perceptions become possible (see Figure 5.2).

Figure 5.2. Eyüp Emre Uçaray's drawing about the liminal stage

THE PATH INTO LIMINALITY

As I wrote in Chapter 4, the liminal state is strongly influenced by the path taken to it. The research I have done for this book, my teaching practice in the Performing Arts Department of Istanbul Bilgi University, and my own experience as an improviser have demonstrated to me that intermodal exercises that focus on low skill and high sensitivity generate critical potential for decentering. And decentering, entering into an imaginary reality through play and art-making, is an effective method for going into the liminal state. Sometimes artists and students who work in performing arts feel that they have taken part in so much movement improvisation that the artistic process no longer makes sense for them. They feel like they have come to a dead end, their range of play reduced and repetitive. In this case, using decentering methods with artistic mediums other than movement to direct the individual into the liminal stage often works well. Their learned technique and habitual choices and aesthetic concerns keep them from exploring and enjoying. When they are directed to another artistic medium in which they have limited experience, new possibilities start opening up. If they approach this medium with a high sensitivity, through the art-making process they are slowly transported into the liminal stage, and they can then also explore this stage with movement. My research with Cansu Kul provided a great example of this.

Cansu is a highly trained dancer and her difficulty is mostly with letting-go. She feels like she is capable of letting-go in her daily life but as she improvises, she has a tendency to rely on movements she is familiar with. In one of our sessions together, I handed her Milan Kundera's *The Unbearable Lightness of Being*, which she had not previously read. I asked her to open random pages for four minutes and write down the words that grabbed her attention. She chose 27 words. I asked her to create a poem drawing that used these words and any extra words of her choice (see Figure 5.3).

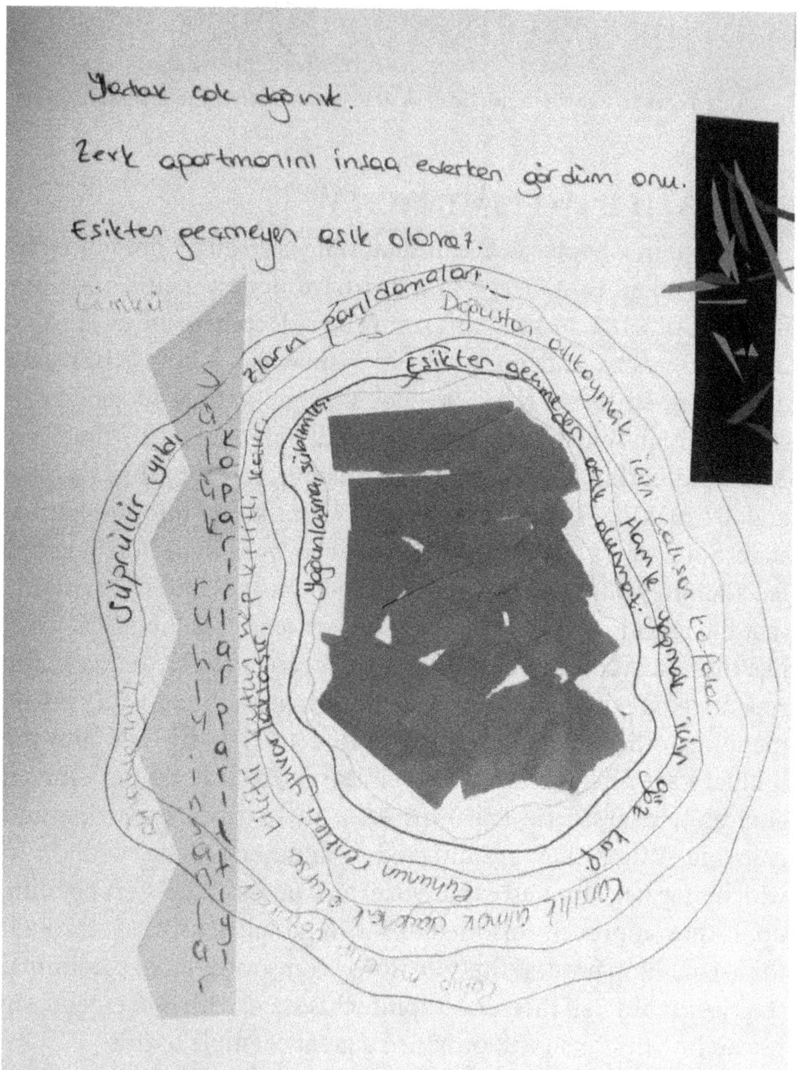

Figure 5.3. Cansu Kul's poem drawing

It was also interesting to observe that the word *threshold* was coming through, because at this point we had not talked about liminality or threshold.

After she completed this poem drawing, I gave Cansu copper paper and some ceramic dough to make a sculpture. We had an open-ended amount of time for our session, and I was trying to load her with as many different tasks as possible to raise her sensitivity to all that surrounded her (words, materials, the air, light, et cetera). Her background is in some ways similar to mine. I started training in classical ballet when I was six years old and began studying modern and jazz dance when I was 11. Therefore, I knew that sometimes when you are technically trained, your concerns about what is correct and beautiful interfere with the flow of the improvisation process. Depending on how one uses it, technique can foster discovery or it can become a prison. Cansu is gifted with a unique, powerful, and passionate energy. She is eager to get excited and when she does, her productive energy flows into everything around her. I aimed to give her a wide variety of exercises that I believed would raise her sensitivity and trigger her productive energy. By the time she completed her sculptures, she had gathered a momentum. I could see that she was ready to feel movement differently and approach it in new ways. I did not want to put her in an open improvisation with no strictures where she could fall into her previous habits. I grabbed four objects made of different materials that she had not used in the sculpture and placed them in the four corners of the studio. Cansu's exercise was to improvise a journey in which she interacted with each element at least once. There was no time limit. It was her call to end the improvisation when she felt that it was complete. In the aesthetic analysis part of our session, Cansu described her process to me:

> I came across two of the materials, the copper paper and the white dough. I didn't go to them intentionally. As I started moving, my eyes were closed and I touched the copper paper somehow but didn't realize it through the touch. I heard the sound it made with the floor as I moved it. I just started playing with it, rather than thinking about how I could move with it. I tried things with it and experienced how it felt on my skin as it touched various parts of

my body. A really strange thing for me was to realize that I had not been moving my arms for some time. I remember the exact moment because I put my weight over my arms and realized it was almost like they were not a part of my body. I was not formulating movement at all. I was sensing and molding… At first when you said 'A Journey,' the thing that came to my mind was a path that as you go through it some things change, transform and at the end you become something else. But I did not think about this as I was moving. My interaction with the copper paper was so interesting that I wanted to add it to me so I put it around my leg, and after I put it on I started doing movements similar to what I was doing in the beginning. It seems like I was interested in experiencing how the same movements would feel with a transformed leg… When I came across the dough, I started sensing the heat in my body. So rather than playing with it in regular ways, I was imagining that the heat of my body was melting it… The strangest thing happened when I came to the fourth object. It was a sheet of paper with a hole in the middle and the hole was almost exactly the shape of the dough that I had melted. I took it and put it over the dough like a surgery cloth. (See Figure 5.4.)

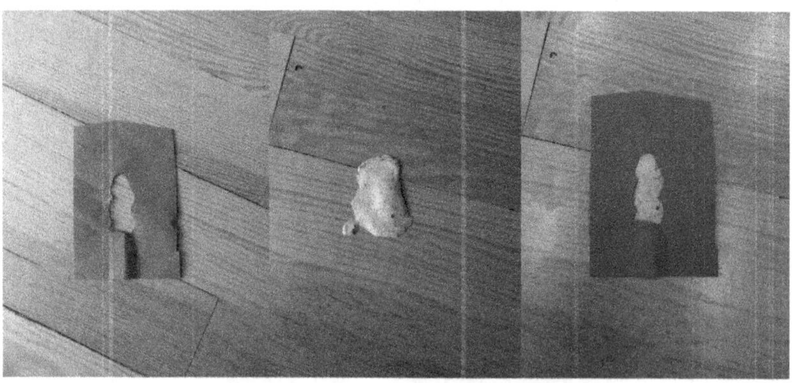

Figure 5.4. The dough and the paper

LIMINAL AS A NO MAN'S LAND

As I improvise, liminality sometimes feels like a no man's land. I make a movement and sometimes a meaning, idea, or feeling is attached to it. When I am not in the liminal, these things that I attach to movement cling to it. As I continue I either go deeper or if I come back to the same movement, it recalls that previous meaning, idea, or the feeling. In the liminal I might experience one feeling, sensation, meaning, or idea the first time I perform that movement and another when I do it again. Neither the ideas that I attach to certain movements nor my perspective are set in stone. I might be very invested in one idea, meaning, or feeling but I can still take a step away and create new ones. This flexibility brings multiplicity, differences, and even oppositions together. I'm not so much disowning one idea as adding a cornucopia of others to it. It becomes a land of freedom with infinite vistas.

In one of my sessions with Sarven Çankar, the multiplicity aspect of liminality surfaced. I asked him to create a sculpture from two human-sized mirrors, five chairs, one wooden pedestal, a green sheet of paper, several purple sticks, and yellow electrical tape. He created a sculpture in which four of the chairs supported the pedestal at table level, placing the sticks and the electrical tape on top (see Figure 5.5).

Figure 5.5. Sarven Çankar's sculpture

In the analysis segment of our session, Sarven explained that as he was making the sculpture, at first he wanted to create a campfire out of the sticks and the tape. He put the cut pieces of the tape aside to use later. But then when the middle part of the stack was able to balance by itself, he decided that he did not need those cut pieces of tape. Then, the moment he thought the sculpture was finished, the stack of campfire wood fell apart. He reproached himself, "See, that is why you had put those pieces of tape aside. You had to make it more stable with them." But when we talked about it afterwards, he said that even though he still regretted the toppled campfire, he was able to see the new arrangement as a group of stars like the Ursa Major. As a witness I could see that this revision did not emerge from an intellect-driven process of pressing himself, "Let's see how I can see this differently." Rather, it was a reflexive idea that almost burst out of him thanks to the liminal state he was in.

Liminality in my experience as an improviser is accompanied by the feeling that you may be the smallest atom in the universe, but there is also a universe in you. It provides the possibility to be macro and micro at the same time. It creates layers and layers of feelings, ideas, concepts, impressions, senses, and meanings... It can open dimensions that you might not have previously even dreamed of.

Part IV

Chaos

While liminality opens up the possibility for chaos to exist, it is up to the improviser and the change agent to transform it into a "productive" or "destructive" chaos. Ellen Levine (quoted in Knill *et al.* 2005) describes productive chaos as an unstructured, disorganized state that fosters vivacity and excitement that something is emerging from the art-making activity that is not yet known. By contrast, destructive chaos refers to a disorganized state that obstructs the art-making activity. In this sense, improvisation offers the possibility of a journey to find new definitions, perspectives, and understandings, as long as the liminal state is achieved and transformed into a productive chaos.

Sometimes the affection for a productive chaos slowly finds its way from the sessions into the lives of the Divers. The realization that it is this chaos that brings together a great rhythm of challenge, satisfaction, passion, nervousness, and excitement slowly sets in. Eyüp Emre Uçaray describes his experience:

> After our sessions my writing process started changing. Most of the time, the notes that I used to take were written in a way that I could not read later on. It was as if my writing tumbled around like my speech. I did not care much about the physicality of the writing process and when I did care about it I was losing the idea that I was thinking about and building. But since our second session, I am writing as if the notebook is listening to me. When I get faster, I try to slow down, thinking about giving time to the notebook to listen to what I am saying. It is like thinking about letting-go and shaping and experiencing another kind of duality. I started to realize that each pen has a different feel to it as well as a sound that it makes as it touches the paper. I am trying to listen to that and think about that touch. This experience both changed the look and the value of my writing. I started going back and reading what I wrote. It used to be a chaos that I did not want to go back to read. Now it is a more clear chaos that does not tire but feeds me.

What does the productivity of the chaos depend on? Many elements, including the participant feeling safe, unjudged, and relaxed in the session environment. Being able to move into a liminal state with high sensitivity in which one experiences the relationship of letting-go and shaping is one of the main critical forces of artistic creation in a productive chaos. In the next section, we go further into the relationship between letting-go and shaping that provides a crucial basis for improvisation in a productive chaos.

PART V

Letting-go and Shaping

The terms letting-go and shaping have meanings that can change according to their relationship to each other. Like the *I* of the *I–Thou* and *I–It*, both terms find their meaning through their relationship.

In order to understand the different meanings these terms come with as their relationship to each other changes, let us imagine a line that makes the shape of infinity. The improviser is like a small shape that can exist in different places on this line of infinity throughout the time she practices (see Figure 5.6). Let us say that the left end of the line represents 100 percent of letting-go and the right end zero percent. The complete opposite is true for shaping. So when a participant is able to attain 90 percent of shaping, she can only let-go at a 10 percent level.

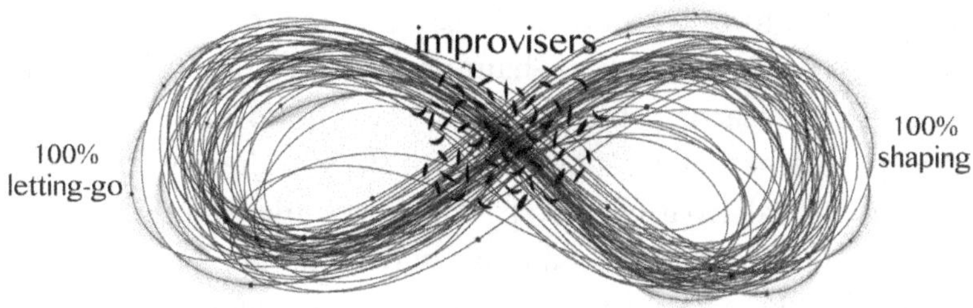

Figure 5.6. Improvisers' letting-go and shaping lines

Often improvisers think that reaching the right or left end points of their line—the 100 percent mark—is unnecessary, especially for the letting-go part. But this is not true. Every point on one's line is valuable, depending on when and for what purpose one uses it.

When a choreographer finishes a piece and looks at it from outside as a whole, she can work more productively with a 90 percent shaping attitude because at this point, shaping involves a deliberative thinking process that brings together all kinds of history and culture, and she can look at the work with this accumulation of references, influences, and markers. For example, she might suddenly realize that the color of a table that she has used on stage inadvertently references a major work in art history and she might not want that reference. This process of realization comes from a cogitating mind. When it comes at these final stages of creating a performance, a sculpture, a drawing, or any artistic work, this cache of references is a valuable resource, but when it surges during the initial improvisations, it breaks the flow of instinctual creating. Improvisation benefits immeasurably from the middle terrain of one's line, where letting-go and shaping can work together and truly transform the medium of the artwork together, whether it be dance, theater, clay, music, or drawing.

As can be seen in Figure 5.6, even in the middle, the improviser does not stand at a fixed point because this kind of disposition would prevent the fluid nature of the relationship. As dancers we are drilled with the importance of posture and retention—making sure the shoulders are not up, holding the stomach in, and pulling up in the thighs. Even the center is sometimes explained like a fist in the stomach that we need to be holding tight. This way of thinking about the body is very structural. Then, as we dance, we are expected to be as fluid as we can be most of the time. As an alternative way of thinking, Shannon Cooney, a highly influential dancer and teacher, incorporates the craniosacral bodywork concept into her contemporary dance classes. Craniosacral bodywork is an "alternative therapy that uses therapeutic touch to manipulate the synarthrodial joints of the cranium" ("Craniosacral therapy," Wikipedia 2016b). According to Cooney, "Its aim is to encourage the vital movement of the craniosacral system to support one's self-regulating healing capacity" (2016). In an interview for this book, Cooney pointed out that holding-based teaching tends to create stiff postures. As an alternative way of thinking, her work concentrates on the craniosacral rhythm of the cerebrospinal fluids. She explained that there is a tidal change in the fluids as they rise and fall. And the fluid midline, in the craniosacral context, is the north and south type of polarity in the body where this rhythm takes place. Fluid midline is in the "neural axis—the central canal of the spinal cord and central axis of the ventricle system within the brain" ("Fluid midline" 2013). And the physical body and the fluid body are oriented in relation to the midline, in the same sense that a compass points north or south based on its current location.

When a compass orients towards north, its needle does not come to a complete stop; it continues to make micro movements.

The idea of not aiming to arrive at a fixed point is also crucial for approaching improvisation. Just as strictly held postures constrict breathing and block movement from flowing, improvisation cannot breathe when the improviser fixates on a position between letting-go and shaping. In order to improvise in some way that "moves" the improviser, letting-go and shaping need to create a fluid relationship. Because the north of this compass constantly changes, one needs to flow with the rhythm to orient to it.

Part VI

The Infinity Line of Letting-go and Shaping

During improvisation it is not possible to only focus on the letting-go aspect of the infinity line of letting-go and shaping without also experiencing the shaping aspect, because so much of what is happening emerges through the interplay of the two. Here we will look at how referencing the two parts makes it easier to see how letting-go and shaping interact in the creative process. The amount of letting-go increases from right to left. The points that are closer to the right side represent the state in which one is more enmeshed in the intellect-driven process (closer to 100 percent shaping), thus realizing the creation in this mode. This positioning on the line is crucial for formulating final observations about a work because the artist here is approaching the work more from her brain than her gut.

If we look at this through the mirror of Martin Buber's *I–It* model (1958), there is a clear *I–It* relation at this point between the artist and the artwork. The artist, in this case the *I* of the *I–It*, through her way of being has placed the artwork apart as an object and therefore separated it from herself. This separation enables her to look at it from a distance. When this occurs during improvisation, though, as opposed to when making final observations about a work near completion, the body usually resorts to movements that have become habitual. It falls back on patterns it has constructed over time and is unable to access what the moment has to offer. Many improvisers from time to time find themselves in this place. For those who are just beginning to improvise, their biggest challenge is usually how to get away from this way of being. This habit of resorting to secure formulas becomes such an opposition to struggle with that even after they find ways to step away from it, they still see it as a dormant enemy, ready to resurface. Most of the epiphanies in this research occurred when the Divers started seeing what the resources of the relationship between shaping and letting-go have to offer.

Another characteristic of this over-thinking mind is that it threatens to take the improviser away from immediate sensations of the studio and into the external world of everyday concerns, the grocery list, pressing errands, what is for dinner... During improvisation these thoughts sometimes surprise the participant and catapult her from the creatively fructuous middle segment of the letting-go and shaping line to the over-controlling right end of the spectrum. Then the mind starts to think even more, thoughts piling upon thoughts, ending with the improviser reproaching herself for being unable to concentrate. Of course this judgment makes it even more difficult to get back into the interplay. The crucial event here is the judgment. One can find ways to transform and even use mental distractions in the improvisation, but once the improviser steps outside and criticizes herself, it becomes much harder to become engaged in the interplay.

In the first few sessions with Gülce Oral, she expressed that this "judging self" had been one of the major problems she had been dealing with for some time. It had become a struggle for her on stage and in life. She often heard the sound of this inner, doubting self that knew her weakest points very well and used them to criticize everything she would do. Then, during our conversation, the potential of seeing this self as the strong shaper and re-channeling this instinct into a more creative channel emerged. Her words suddenly changed:

> It feels really good to think about shaping this way. Because it can also be the side that looks from the outside. It judges the work and the self. And I always saw it as a negative thing. Something that I wanted to silence. Something I wanted to get rid of. And of course as I paid more attention to it, its voice increased. It was being fed greatly by my desire to disown it. But now thinking about it as a shaping influence leads me to see it as a resource that enables me to make aesthetic choices.

The hectic, multi-tasking everyday pace of our times conspires to maintain us in this state of dense, constant, often frenzied and breathless thinking. Our minds thus over-engaged, we fall into the trap of thinking all questions can only be resolved by the intellect. We tend to disregard the sensations of the body and its instinctive thinking mechanism. The body cannot be completely disregarded because it is always processing, but its full potential is often overlooked. Its capabilities and resources are being put aside.

I have been teaching contemporary dance movement technique classes to first-year Performing Arts students with different backgrounds at Istanbul Bilgi University for the past ten years. Each year the same thing happens. In the second semester of the class, I tell the students that they will be creating a solo choreography. They bring ideas, we talk about them, and get them to a point where they can physically start playing with those ideas. No sooner have I told them that they have the entire class time to work on the piece, with the goal of presenting something by the end of the period, that they all sit down. I wait for 10 to 15 minutes and then ask them what they are doing. They look at me with confused faces, and one of them tells me that they are choreographing. Their minds are at work, imagining movement, and their bodies are as stiff as pistachio shells. They forget that they can think with movement, drawing, and playing in order to create movement, because up until this point in their lives (mostly because of the education system in Turkey) they have only approached creation as an intellect-driven process. As all the Divers have been my students in the past, they have lived through this moment. Gökdağ Yalçın recalls that this realization completely changed his perspective and transformed his way of searching for ideas. But even after this epiphany, he admitted, the urge to stay at the high end of the shaping/low end of the letting-go in the line remains powerful. Even when he is dreaming, this urge comes up, shaping itself into different forms. Sometimes he realizes that he is dreaming, but cannot wake up. Sometimes a character steps forth and tries to take him to a place in the dream where he can let-go. Usually Gökdağ resists this offer and chooses not to go.

The other end of the line spectrum is where letting-go is near 100 percent and shaping near zero. Sometimes when experiencing something at this level of sensitivity one might not even remember it at all. This happened to me once during a performance. The choreography was set in an asylum and I was portraying one of the patients. I had a solo that shook me up each time I danced it. In one of the performances, I woke up suddenly in the wings and asked the other dancers if I had already danced the solo and the other parts because I could see from what was happening on stage that those segments had already happened. They told me that I had, and that it had been a really good performance. I had no recollection of this. I even realized that one of my contact lenses had fallen out. I completed the performance and never quite figured out what had happened.

In *Landscape of the Now*, Kent de Spain writes about "tracking" (2014). He explains that during the course of improvisation, it is important that the improviser keeps track of certain aspects of what is happening to her in order to use them in making choices. This is a vital tool for shaping. At the far left end of the line, where there is an extreme level of letting-go, there is no possibility of tracking. Therefore one loses a valuable tool for feeding one's improvisations and also cannot use the improvisation as a resource for a choreographic project. After this extreme state of letting-go, the improviser is left without even the smallest memory of what has happened.

Part VII

Letting-be

The middle of the line of letting-go and shaping is the playground—the segment in which one feels awakened, enriched, resourceful, and alive. The description of this kind of existence and creativity in the moment changes from person to person. I choose to call it "diving into" the moment while two of the many other variations are "being in" or "leaving oneself in the moment." No matter what it is called, diving into the moment is different from existing exclusively in that moment. While existing exclusively in the moment is a form of letting-go, diving into it combines letting-go and shaping. The meanings of both letting-go and shaping evolve in this realm. Letting-go is not a state of existence in which one risks losing one's memory. Shaping does not involve constantly thinking, talking to oneself, and processing. Their interplay fosters new meanings and carries the improviser into "letting-be."

"Letting-be" in its composite form is a blend of surrendering, sensing, suggesting, and constructing. It is an active presence that is, in reality, almost effortless. It is a letting-go with all the senses awake and listening to the art that wants to emerge. But the moment also exists in the context that was carried through the moments that preceded it. So it is not fully letting-go (because one is not letting-go of the immediate past). Stephen Levine notes that "letting-be requires the presence of the artist, and, in the critical revision of what arrives, even a conscious and deliberate presence" (quoted in Knill *et al.* 2005, p.42). Shaping, an act of understanding and using the sources of those preceding moments and other influences to give form, is also part of "diving into the moment" and therefore the state of letting-be.

Each individual, whether a professional or an amateur, describes the state of letting-be in her own unique way. There is no one ultimate place to be reached or one experience that can be taught but rather, individual ways of living in this state. And with time, if the improviser remains open to new experiences, even those ways can expand their variety.

I see the visualizations of these states like portals. They provide a glimpse of a unique experience and then take you back to your reality with that enhanced perspective. In my case as a Diver, my reality has been enriched by going through the portals of the other Divers, leaving me feeling like there is infinite room for mine to grow, transform, and change. Before I undertook this research, I was so filled with joy in my own visualization of letting-be that it felt like I did not need a different image for the rest of my life. When I listened to the Divers, though, and sensed in many ways their different descriptions, I came to realize that I was, in a way, limiting my imagination and holding on to one exclusive visual model too inflexibly. I still currently describe my existence when I dive into the moment with this visual model, but now I approach the experience of letting-be with a more malleable disposition.

Before I go into some of the results of the Divers' fruitful imaginations and experiences, I will start with my own imagery for reflecting the feeling of letting-be. In the previous chapter I described my *Passage* as a labyrinth, with an amazing lake surrounded by different types of greens at its center. Smaller lakes are spread around different parts of the labyrinth. Going through *the Passage* entails going through various paths in the labyrinth and arriving at a lake. Diving into the moment is like jumping into that lake. As different parts of my body touch the water, my body becomes water. At the same time, I am the water, I feel it around me. So it is as if there is an object–subject relationship and a oneness at the same time. This also ties into the "wholeness" idea I wrote about in Chapter 2, a wholeness that can capture multiplicity, differences, and even oppositions and just be. In this kind of letting-be, I do make conscious decisions and realize them through shaping. It is not a distracting, intellect-driven process; it is an experience of being a whole. In this state, my other visual image, the two heads of the dragon (one being letting-go and the other shaping), find a way to exist and work together in such a productive way that a radiance flows through their body and wings due to this connection. They achieve more than what they could achieve working separately. Their wholeness enables them to sense anything that approaches them together, for example, a gust of wind, and to react to it as a whole.

Gülce Oral describes letting-go and shaping as melting into each other in her experience of letting-be:

> When I dive into the moment I feel like I am shaping while being in the state of existence of letting-go. They become really hard to differentiate from one another. It feels as if a new dimension opens up in the space. The space gets distorted. As if I am looking through a fish-eye lens. The space becomes more circular. The borders lose their acuteness. And sometimes, I also see creatures and things. I communicate with them, as in a dream. But the whole space does not transform into somewhere else. I am still here and I am aware of it.

For some people the visual image that accompanies letting-be is not just of their existence but also encompasses the space around them. Gökdağ Yalçın describes this in spatial terms:

> For me being in the moment is like this: There is a 500-meter-long corridor, 2 meters wide, with curtains that you can tear and go through. In the first 100 meters there is a 10-meter space between each curtain. In the next 100 there is a 5-meter space. In the next, 1 meter. In the next, 50 centimeters. And in the final 100 meters, only 10 centimeters. When you are moving through them, when you are tearing the curtains, you get a strong feeling. In the final 100 meters, you are immersed in that feeling and you don't even notice the space and the curtains.
>
> Time is something that you lose as you start thinking about it. I believe that being in the moment is like this: you step out of it, the moment you become aware of it. So the time or the moment is not something that is outside of you, it is the sensation that you get when you tear that curtain. Gödel [Kurt Gödel, 1906–1978, the well-known, Austrian and later American logician, mathematician and philosopher] talks about a mathematical theory. He understands time like this: imagine somebody who is lighting a torch in a dark night outside. If he would turn it in a circular way we would see it as a circle of light. But in reality it is made up of flashing moments. Because our eyes don't perceive the moments in between, we see it as a whole. This is how we understand time. We perceive it as a whole but it proceeds as 'tick

> tick tick' in reality. Maybe we are in the moment when we perceive and shape the ticks.

For some, letting-be is what enables a completely different perception of time—an opportunity for seconds to really expand and for a new dimension to open up. For others, even if the letting-be state releases them from constantly thinking about time, their internal clock can still be working. In *Landscape of the Now*, de Spain (2014, p.46) describes the ability to measure time without being enslaved to it as follows:

> Tracking time helps me know where I am in this particular performance and approximately when to bring it to a close. Now, it is not like I'm constantly thinking, How long did *that* take, how long did *that* take? But over the course of the moving, some part of my awareness is occasionally acknowledging the passage of time, and as I approach my sense of twenty minutes, that awareness moves closer to consciousness and I suddenly 'know' it is time to look for an ending.

Another Diver who loses the perception of time is Cansu Kul, who emphasizes that she does not so much dive into the moment as find it:

> I express it as I found myself in the moment. It is as if there is an energy line that surrounds the body. It is like the 'loading' line when you are downloading a page on the internet. This line draws me like a body of light and when I'm in this state, my perception of time disappears. I become the real me. I do things with a different kind of consciousness that feels very much in control but is also unconscious.

Öykü Oktay's description of her experience parallels Cansu's:

> It is like a certain movement of a baby. Whenever I describe a baby I make this movement. The feet are up and the baby is sitting down. Being in the moment means feeling like I am doing this movement in the air. There is a feeling of easiness to it. It is like there is a huge empty space without gravity around me and as if I am doing a movement that is extremely comfortable. Like when children concentrate on something, and are so focused on it that

> they have this impression on their face of true happiness. Being in the moment is like that, a silly happiness. But even though it is like being a baby, it also is like being a giant baby who takes up a good amount of space. It is not a place where you are little and insecure. It is sympathetic.

Experiencing the state of letting-be through the interplay of letting-go and shaping transforms the individual, not just as an improviser in the arts, but also as an improviser of life. The key to this transformation is in understanding the receptive nature of this relationship.

Part VIII

Etken and *Edilgen*

As explained earlier in Chapter 2, the idea of wholeness I address in this book involves creating a togetherness that includes multiplicity, differences, and even oppositions. Because "wholeness" is a concept that can encapsulate multiple meanings, how this plays out varies from individual to individual. The same variety of elements is already inherently present in the disparate qualities of the self, but for me, erecting a liquid, changeable, and soft frame around these elements produces a sense of peace. It enables me to embrace them as the ingredients that constitute the variety in me, rather than seeing them as fragmented components. Therefore seeing all of these components as a whole also means making peace with a vision of the self in which opposing ideas, drives, and feelings co-exist. Without this understanding we are trying to reach a utopian state of purity that does not fully utilize or realize human potential. Humans grow from their oppositions and their learned ability to find ways for these oppositions to co-exist. The relationship between letting-go and shaping presents a clear example of this concept.

When we look at the relationship of letting-go and shaping during the course of improvisation, we recognize moments in which one of these drives is more dominant than the other. For example, as I let-go I open myself up to movements that are not part of my standard repertory. As these inspirations emerge, I can shape them and turn them into motifs, play with their levels, sizes, rhythms, and adapt them to the movement style of different body parts. This is a state in which letting-go and shaping work together rather than struggling against each other. It is not as if one becomes active and the other passive. Even if one of them is actively determining the movement mode in a given moment, the other is not completely passive; it is more nuanced than this. To understand these nuances, it is instructive to look at the Turkish approximations of the English words "active" and "passive," which do not have exactly the same meanings. While *etken,* the Turkish word for active, is defined as "the power that has an effect, the one that has determining power" (Püsküllüoğlu 1994a), *edilgen*, the closest equivalent to the English "passive," means "the one who is affected by what is done" (Püsküllüoğlu 1994b). While "passive" is an explanation for a state that can exist by itself, *edilgen* is a state that needs its opposite *etken* and the possibility of some kind of action, movement, or effect in order to exist. So in this way the meaning of *edilgen* is closer to the English word "receptive" than "passive." When letting-go and shaping engage in interplay, they conduct a reflexive relationship of being *etken* and *edilgen*, or active and passive/receptive. They unite in the moment, with neither of them becoming completely "passive." When one of them becomes *edilgen*, it actively lets itself be affected by what is being received. In this receptive stage, it actually sorts what to take in and how to incorporate what it takes in. In its own *apparently* passive existence, the letting-go or the shaping part of the artist is receptive and therefore active in another respect.

The two heads in my dragon image (see Figure 1.1) symbolize letting-go and shaping. They maneuver to control one body. Both are wild and because of this nature at first they both want to be the decision-maker. They want to control the improviser and carry her to a point of 100 percent letting-go or 100 percent shaping. They are determined. Each one is filled with a feeling of superiority and a desire to be in charge. After a period of going up against each other, the heads realize that the monopolizing of control by one or the other of the movement of the body they share is not that practical. While they are flying, if one of them goes into being completely passive rather than being *edilgen*, the other needs to carry more of the body weight. So being in complete power without the other one is like trying to fly while a weight pulls the body down to the earth. On the other hand, if both of them want to be active but pull in different directions at the same time, they are still wasting energy. They cannot just divide the body, and the conflict disables them from going anywhere. But when they realize that they can turn this dissension into an interplay, something amazing happens. All of a sudden, they become capable of doing even more things than the sum of what they can accomplish alone. Symbolizing this idea is the visual image at the beginning of this book: a two-headed dragon on which each head has an individual wing. Between them is a nerve center. Through the interplay of the two heads and their individual wings in this nerve center, new, shared censors appear and the two heads of the dragon are able to find their relationship. And the core of this relationship is receptivity.

Receptivity is not exclusive to being *edilgen*. Due to its relation with *edilgen*, *etken* can also be receptive. Whether it is activated in letting-go or shaping, the receptivity of the *etken* is almost the same. When a party becomes *etken* in a relationship, it is given a lot of power and the option to decide how to use it. With the Divers I discussed how easy it is to slide into the path of abusing this power. For example, when one improvises and shaping becomes *etken*, if not guided, it sometimes tries to transform the improvisation into preconceived movements. It is only when the *etken* (whether letting-go or shaping) also becomes receptive, senses the other, and knows when to yield its position to *edilgen* that a path to a state of letting-be, where letting-go and shaping can work together, is opened up. As long as the authority that is granted to the *etken* does not blind the eyes of its current owner, whether that is letting-go or shaping, the potential for interplay exists. In a session following one in which we had discussed *etken* and *edilgen* states of being in both letting-go and shaping, Gülce Oral enthusiastically shared an experience that she had had a few days earlier. She pointed out that after a period of contemplating letting-be, in one of her theater performances she opened the gates of the barrage:

> And I did this at the point where I always had the biggest difficulty. Something that made me feel so real came to me. It was something that was full and could contain everything. It also brought a desire to cry. But I knew that the character would not really cry so I redirected the strength of that feeling to laughing.

In her experience, Gülce was overcome by a strong sensation of letting-go. This was something that had previously eluded her. Even though she is known as an actress with great sensitivity and openness to letting-go, for some time she had been unable to access that part of her. So when she felt it resurging, it was cherry blossom time. Letting-go was completely *etken* in her existence. As she realized that the character she was portraying would not be likely to behave in the way that letting-go was suggesting, her real strength emerged. She did not stay with the *etken* drive that was already in charge (in letting-go) or just switch to shaping and disregard the urge that letting-go had inspired. While she let her previously *edilgen* drive, shaping, become the *etken* drive, she "kept" the strength of the feeling that letting-go had ushered in, simply shaping it into another form.

In and of itself it might even be harder for the *etken* drive to promote openness and sensitivity, because when letting-go or shaping becomes *etken*, it is in the most powerful state it can reach alone. But with time and practice, if they can increase their sensitivity while they are being *etken*, the equation starts to change. Both letting-go and shaping realize that as they become *etken*, their sensitivity to the other carries them further into learning, finding, and experiencing new things.

The receptivity imparted by *edilgen* is a bit different. As letting-go and shaping become *edilgen*, they are taken into a position where they have less impact on molding the improvisation or the creative process—but they are not in any way passive. Their sensitivity is acute, and they are engaged in everything that is happening. For example, I think my shaping part is a very good memorizer. While it is *edilgen*, it gives letting-go room to flow freely but keeps track of all the movements and makes proposals for recalling those movements later on. It can be said that being *edilgen* is also like going through a phase of pre-shaping. *Edilgen* means being receptive, present to the *etken* and open to being influenced. In this way, it is actually "embracing" the other, in Buber's terms. Buber uses two different words in two different publications to explain the same notion: embracing and inclusion. Both terms apply to adopting "the other's lived reality without in any way forfeiting one's own" (quoted in Gordon 2011, p.212). Instead of being *edilgen* in the full sense of the term, which includes being receptive, if one falls into being simply passive, the whole system falls apart because the embrace gets broken. This reciprocal sensitivity connection gets scrambled. And this disconnection cuts the improviser's play range in half. So the *edilgen* in a different way holds as much power as the *etken*.

In the state of letting-be, where letting-go and shaping fuse, *edilgen* and *etken* embrace each other. The separation between the two blurs and sometimes even disappears. They are both separate and also one. They are truly present to each other. The *I–Thou* relationship that letting-go and shaping build through being *etken* and *edilgen* is so direct that letting-go and shaping get to know each other "clearer than all the clearness of the world" (Buber 1958, p.10). The interplay at this point is flowing so freely that the improviser finds herself in the unique state of letting-be without being preoccupied by questions of letting-go and shaping.

In his experience as a tango dancer and teacher, Gökdağ Yalçın expressed that the letting-be state that is achieved through the evolving relationship of *etken* and *edilgen* is essential in tango. Even though technically there seems to be a leader, the man, and a follower, the woman, for advanced dancers the relationship is not that simple. He explained that sometimes the woman reads the lead of the man in a different way than the man intends and moves in a different direction than he anticipated. If the man can go with this, he can follow her lead rather than trying to repair it. If this process continues and gets faster, then eventually there is no leader or follower. The separation blurs and the roles change and change without the two people noticing it. A similar experience happens in the mirror game that is used both in dance and theater classes. The students are paired up. Even though the instructor designates the leader at the beginning, the goal is accomplished when the performers by themselves eventually decide, without words, to shift the lead. They eventually become so in synch that an observer cannot guess who is leading.

Effectively channeling, deploying, and balancing the respective energies of *etken* and *edilgen* is the key to transforming letting-go and shaping from competitors into collaborators. In this state of letting-be, letting-go and shaping are able to both maximize their own individual potentials and create a new "whole" together, like the *I–Thou* relation that is larger than the sum of the two parts. Whether they are in *etken* or *edilgen* dispositions of varying degrees, letting-go and shaping start to nurture each other. The increasing harmony of their interplay lifts them to new grounds.

Part IX

Art and Life

Before I started the writing phase of this book I went into the dance studio one day. I moved and moved and moved. I felt like I was engaging in a contact improvisation with someone, an intense one, but there was not anyone else really there. I lay down on the floor looking at the ceiling and could feel my imagined partner's face on my hand. I dreamed of a beautiful sky beyond the ceiling. Bright and sunny with white clouds. Without any words coming out of my mouth, I told my imaginary partner that I was pregnant. She said that she knew. We were pregnant together with something amazing. We were in sync. A tear fell from her eye. It continued to glide past her cheek and into my hand as if there were no distinction between our bodies. Our existence had a rhythm that united us. We were together. Later I realized that this other being was always in me; she was my letting-be.

When one experiences the interplay between letting-go and shaping and finds different ways of balancing the two rather than leaving them in constant battle over who is in charge, this disposition can be applied to one's whole life. This is not just a method of improvisation but also a concept for communicating deeply. It is a way of respecting differences and using them as resources rather than constantly seeing them in opposition. In creating a relationship, the attitude is critical. While letting-go or shaping is *etken*, if it sees the other as passive and does not approach in a sensitive manner, it breaks the flow. If, while in the *edilgen* state, either one sees itself as exclusively passive, this can also break the flow. The key is to maintain the sensitivity that keeps letting-go and shaping attuned to each other so that they can better work together in letting-be.

In 1998 I read an inspiring poem by Murathan Mungan, *A Solitary Opera* (1992). In one of our sessions, Gökdağ shared a translation of a remark by Montaigne that he found inspiring: "A good poem does not satisfy the human mind but convulses it." (Unfortunately I could not locate any English resources that verify the accuracy of this quote, but I found it touching and therefore wanted to mention it here.) Mungan's poem has had this effect on me every time I have read it. He wrote the poem over the course of a year, and the theme is based on a break-up. As the 16-page work progresses, Mungan's feelings and thoughts are transformed.

This therapeutic aspect of art is fed when one invites both letting-go and shaping to create a work together. Their collaborative, sensitive approach to each other provides a path for change, healing, and new perspectives. It enlarges the range of play and matures the artist. Shaping benefits from the freeing influence of letting-go that can bring in fresh movement. Letting-go benefits from the gathering, organizing ability of shaping. When a performer is able to create an interplay between *etken* and *edilgen* in her artistic process of fusing and balancing letting-go and shaping, then, slowly, applying this approach to life becomes possible. It is like a slit that is opened up in a completely dark space. The light slowly starts to filter in to both her artistic and everyday life. As she realizes the changes that light creates, she becomes eager to enlarge the slit and let the light flow.

CHAPTER 6

THE ESSENCE

The sea was unfriendly to you.
It may only be mirror-smooth when rest is an articulation of its life.

Karl Jaspers (from Biemel and Saner 2003, p.103)

"*Der schwer gefaßte Entschluß*" ("The Difficult Decision"), the fourth movement of Beethoven's String Quartet No. 16, *Opus 135*, is built on two motifs. The first asks, "*Muss es sein*?" ("Must it be?"), to which the second immediately responds, twice: "*Es muss sein*" ("It must be") (see Figure 6.1).

Figure 6.1. The two motifs that appear at the fourth movement of Beethoven's String Quartet No. 16 (Opus 135). *Image re-created by Büşra Erçin*

Improvisation is like an immense ocean with many approaching shores. There is a near infinity of possible departure points. In the research and writing phase of this book, when concepts took form I made a point of asking myself "*Muss es sein*?" What follows are the concepts that I believe to be the "*muss sein*"s of an improvisation if letting-go and shaping are to enter into an interplay in which they can constantly revolve between being *etken* and *edilgen* and transport the improviser to a state of letting-be.

AWARENESS

In *Flow*, psychology professor Mihayl Csikszentmihalyi talks about "joy, creativity, [and] the process of total involvement with life" he calls "flow" (1990, p.xi; see also Csikszentmihalyi 1996). Csikszentmihalyi outlines six distinctive features of the flow experience. The first is exceptionally important for the improvisation process:

> The experience of merging action and awareness: There is no dualism in 'flow'; while an actor may be aware of what he is doing, he cannot be aware that he is aware—if he is, there is a rhythmic, behavioral, or cognitive break. Self-consciousness makes him stumble. 'Flow' perceived from the 'outside' becomes non-'flow' or anti-'flow.' Pleasure gives way to problems, to worry, to anxiety. (quoted in Turner 1979, p.56)

The awareness of "being aware" takes the improviser completely out of letting-go and breaks the rhythm of the improvisation. This happens often, especially to those new to improvisation. As the improviser matures, not only does she start experiencing these cognitive breaks less but she also becomes able to transform them. She finds ways to slowly fade into the middle segment of the letting-go and shaping line rather than getting anxious about living this break and worrying about how to solve it. A highly sensitive and resourceful improviser, Hasan Canberk Karaçay, stated that for him, this shift is natural.

> If while improvising I realize that my shirt is wet, I don't go into the mode in which I say, 'Oh, I need to change my shirt' and I don't deny this realization or try to take myself away from there either. Rather I see it, realize it and challenge myself: 'Okay, this is sweat, what do I do with it, how do I improvise with this realization, where can it take me?'

In improvisation we want to be sensitive to all that surrounds us. We want to be aware. We just do not want our awareness to break our flow. For example, we can see the audience members and notice the looks on their faces, we can imagine how we look from the outside, but the line between using this awareness to build our flow and letting it break the flow is thin. This awareness of the audience or a change in our body like sweat or a noise (such as a cell phone ringing) can become a distraction. This happens mostly for two reasons, both linked to our own attitude: one, if the disturbance or perturbation comes from our fellow performers, the problem may be that we zoned them out ahead of time, excluding them from our space; two, if it comes from our fellow performers and/or the audience, we may have decided beforehand that they would remain constant unless we, by our own action, changed them. When the improviser predetermines her awareness in this manner, she closes herself to the variety of potential energies, movements, and sounds of the others that surround or observe (to encompass the audience) her. If we open ourselves to taking into account these potentials, then we will have the option to either acknowledge them and continue with what we were working on before, unaltered, or integrate them into our improvisation. This way, awareness becomes a resource that can potentially enrich our improvisation. When this conscious awareness is transformed into a resource, then the improviser does not go into the state that Csikszentmihalyi describes as "being aware that you are aware" (quoted in Turner 1979). She just remains aware.

An adaptable disposition is crucial because, as the word improvisation clearly communicates, when an improviser starts out on this journey, she does not know what is going to come her way. The beauty lies in the mystery of it. The improviser needs to start out with a commitment not to judge herself even when she lets her flow get interrupted. Only then does she become enabled to transform these interruptions into something useful, at the same time lessening their impact by depriving them of their gravity.

SURRENDER

For improvisation, most of my students think that they should totally surrender to letting-go and only then will they be able to improvise in a satisfactory manner. I find this not to be true. The idea of surrendering completely in letting-go is to stow the self away, which is both impossible and unproductive. We try so hard to fill ourselves with information and experience; why, then, in improvisation are we so afraid of shaping that takes its power from all this accumulated knowledge? Is it because we hear it too much? Is it because we are afraid that this stock of knowledge could block out the new experiences that can emerge? Would it disturb us as much if we approached our shaping side with care in a spirit of understanding and negotiation? What would happen if, rather than shrinking before this force or trying to quiet its voice, we helped our shaping side become more receptive to letting-go?

What if, rather than feeling she has to choose between surrendering to letting-go or to shaping, the improviser decided to surrender to receptivity? If she can do this, then both letting-go and shaping will find ways to create an interplay and be able to realize their full potential. Surrendering to receptivity is the key to reaching a state of letting-be (the state in which letting-go and shaping rotate between being *etken* and *edilgen* and create an interplay). Then, at that state, letting-go can bring in all the creative materials, ideas, feelings, and new concepts that can be played with, while shaping can bring in ideas and learned or pre-existing concepts of ways to construct and re-construct all of these into new forms.

Let us return to the approach advocated by Martin Buber. Victor Turner, an interpreter of the philosopher in the field of cultural anthropology, explains that:

> Martin Buber's notions of the I–Thou relationship and the Essential We formed by people moving towards a freely chosen common goal are intuitive perceptions of a non-transactional order or a quality of human relationship, in the sense that people do not necessarily initiate action towards one another in the expectation of a reaction that satisfies their interest. (Turner 1982, p.46)

When we look at the relationship of letting-go and shaping as an *I–Thou* relationship, we realize that in order to get clear of any expectations and move towards a common goal, both forces in us (letting-go and shaping) need to open up their sensitivity and surrender to receptivity.

When letting-go or shaping are in the *edilgen* state, rather than being passive they need to be receptive, open to being affected by what the other brings in, watching over the process, and collecting ideas, feelings, concepts, and thoughts. The idea of surrendering to receptivity is easier to grasp and accomplish at the state of being *edilgen*.

When letting-go or shaping are in the *etken* state at different times of their interplay, they should also be willing to listen, sense, and receive all the information that the other is communicating. Even though surrendering is a word that often has a negative connotation, surrendering to receptivity can be seen as an act of empowerment. In one of our sessions, Eyüp Emre Uçaray told me that he had recently been thinking a lot about the forces of letting-go and shaping in his daily life. So the next time he improvised, in one of our sessions, he started making different sounds while he was breathing in and out. He was standing still with his eyes closed, and the sounds that he created in the two different parts of a breath cycle sounded like a dialogue. When he spoke about this after he finished improvising, he explained that it felt like these were the voices of letting-go and shaping. One would speak as he breathed in and the other when he breathed out. As he shared this sentiment, I realized that for Emre, letting-go and shaping were circulating the breath between each other. They were finding new ways through their own methods of formation for how the breath might sound and how to listen to it.

When letting-go and shaping are both receptive throughout their interplay, this receptivity enables them to join their forces and create with an incredible sense of flow. Then and only then can the art-making surrender to them. Or, as Salvador Dalí once wrote to Federico García Lorca:

> ...What we must do is search our poetry energetically and virtuously so that it will surrender to us. We need to have forgotten poetry completely before it can fall naked into our arms. [It's a sort of] state of poetic alert. What poetry cannot hear is indifference. Indifference is the Devil's armchair. But it is indifference we hear babbling in the streets, dressed grotesquely in self-satisfaction and culture. (Dalí and Lorca 2004)

SAFETY AND THE THIRD WAY

In Expressive Arts (EXA), the change agent "can be thought of as the holder of the space, but only if holding is understood as a setting-free for the realization of one's possibilities" (Levine, quoted in Knill *et al.* 2005, p.72). The student, patient, or client needs to feel free to take risks and to find ways for unexpected moments to emerge from these risks. As the change agent for the one-to-one sessions with the Divers, I was the one who had the option and also the responsibility to set the values of the space that would enable the Divers to feel relaxed, free, and unjudged. In this role, I learned the importance of supporting the Divers in various ways so that they could step outside of their safety zones. The most effective support is the affirmation that something new, the third way (Knill, Barba, and Fuchs 2004), can emerge from artistic play in the situation of the two (the Diver and the change agent). Knill describes this new way as the "surprising openings that lead to clarity and solutions. They are also described as 'Aha-experiences'" (quoted in Knill *et al.* 2005, p.134). When the Diver has already experienced this emergence directly, she can hold on to the knowledge thus acquired and modify her expectations accordingly. But when she has not experienced the third way yet, then it is up to me as the change agent to communicate that decentering (going beyond the focused theme into the imaginary realm through art-making) makes it possible for the third way to emerge. And in order for any improviser to experience the third way, she needs to feel safe to take risks, to look or feel foolish, to fall physically or emotionally. In other words, she needs to feel safe to be unsafe and to walk the road described by Dalí:

> I don't believe in the seated artist but in the one who is walking the road. The imagination is a spiritual apparatus, a luminous explorer of the world it discovers. The imagination fixes and gives clear life to fragments of the invisible reality where man is stirring… (Dalí and Lorca 2004)

Once the Divers experience this refreshing sense of it being okay to not have the solutions right away, to be in a stage of searching, to be skillfully lost in their improvisations, then they of course want to import this feeling into their other artistic processes. Eyüp Emre

Uçaray and I had been talking about this concept for some time even before our sessions together. Then, in one of our sessions, he said that, unfortunately, the actors he worked with usually expected him as the director to be omniscient, and this expectation did not allow him the opportunity to go through his own journey of being unsafe:

> Because the actor feels that he is in chaos, lost and searching, he wants me to be the anchor. This is an understanding that suggests that the director's purpose for being there is to know and answer all the questions. Even before any rehearsals his ideas about what is going to happen should be clear. It is as if the rehearsal process is only for the actors. Of course I prepare and come with ideas. But I also have to be in a state where I feel safe to throw all of those ideas into the garbage. I find that keeping quiet most of the time and when I speak asking questions rather than making comments tend to work best at those moments.

I believe that Emre's solution works well for him because he shares his creative process with the assistant directors. But if he can form a company (I truly anticipate that he will be doing this in the near future) of artists able to explore territory outside their safety zones together in order to empower the artistic process, then he will find the model he is searching for.

In the *I–Thou* relationship, two beings open themselves up to each other and create the space in between them in order to form a bridge and have an encounter. In Chapter 5 I described how these two parties can also represent the letting-go and shaping forces in one being and create this encounter by finding an interplay through being *etken* and *edilgen*. This encounter enables the *third* way to emerge. In the example above, while the encounter might be happening between the internal letting-go and shaping forces of both the director and the actor, it also needs to be happening between these two people. The space in between two different performers is created by both parties. The same is true of the relationship between a director and an actor. Only when the space is filled by both of them can their bridge support both their internal encounters of the interplay between letting-go and shaping and their collaborative, interpersonal encounters. Their mutual support for feeling safe to be unsafe will provide space for the *third* way to emerge.

DOUBT

My three-and-a-half-year-old son, Ali Emre, is a big fan of spinning, whirling, and any movement that involves turning. He and I frequently dance contact improvisation all around our home (mostly he prefers the kitchen), and at some point in the process he always takes my hand and starts us turning together. It is almost always me who stops our turning because I get nauseous after spinning for five minutes. (When spinning, five minutes can feel like an eternity.) One time he told me that I did not know how to really spin—that I was "looking and seeing too much." I could not understand the meaning of what he was saying, but it stayed with me. Since I was trained in ballet from an early age, my idea of turning was directly linked with finding a point to focus on and turning my neck fast enough to return to that point. While performing a manège (a ballet term applied to a series of steps or turns executed while circling the stage; see American Ballet Theatre no date) I would change that point after each turn but still keep a fixed point. But it was impossible to maintain this technique in spinning.

With this challenge on my mind, I was excited when I saw that Ziya Azazi was giving a workshop called "Dervish in Progress" in Istanbul. Azazi is a dancer, choreographer, and teacher whose work focuses on spinning and whirling. His technical facility is astonishing. On the first day of the workshop, Azazi explained that as we spin we only perceive our surroundings generally, as light and color, meaning in part that it is impossible to perceive them in their details, or to fix one identifiable point. He stated that if we try to identify clear images of our surroundings, we break the flow of the spinning. So we have to convince our minds before we start that as we spin this generalized visual information will be enough to keep us going. (So what my son actually meant was that my vision was too active. That his perception of his surroundings when he spun was more generalized probably explains why he was not getting nauseous, even after spinning for 10 minutes, and I was.) I believed in my teacher. I did everything as he suggested and I was really surprised by the amazing feeling of simplicity that started to grow in me as I spun for hours. As Heidegger says: "The more simple things become, the more difficult it will be to think and to say anything appropriate about them" (quoted in Biemel and Saner 2003). The only thing that disturbed this sublime clarity was doubt. During the millisecond that I doubted, everything fell apart. My mind tried to harness a still, fixed, clear image of my surroundings and in order to do that, it broke the rhythm that I had built up. Instead of coming to a peaceful stop, my body dragged, fell, and became sick. The flowing feeling of simplicity was crushed to pieces. All of this happened because of doubt. And going through an experience in which the deleterious effects of this second-guessing on my physical and spiritual equilibrium were so clear and traumatic helped me understand the importance of freeing myself from doubts.

We may not always realize this, but we are liable to experience distractions and breaks of flow similar to mine in spinning when we succumb to doubt while improvising. Hasan Canberk Karaçay explained that for him, being in the moment "is like a process of disposal. Letting-go of the excess. A process of becoming simple, like carving away to the essential. Getting rid of the unnecessary loads. Not doubting your technical skills." In our conversations, Canberk said that doubt sometimes impeded his creative flow. In another session while we were in a garden, he reported that as he was working on the sculpture I had assigned, images and shapes were coming to him but he immediately started questioning and doubting these visuals. Where were they coming from? Was he recalling something he had actually seen? He acknowledged that he needed to leave these doubts behind in order to really work. In my opinion, such self-questioning can become a resource for the artist when she is past the improvisation stage and ready to evaluate the finished work. During improvisation, however, they do nothing but stop her from playing.

Pediatrician and psychoanalyst D.W. Winnicott, in *Home Is Where We Start From*, states:

> To be creative a person must exist and have a feeling of existing, not in conscious awareness, but as a basic place to operate from. Creativity is then the doing that arises out of being. It indicates

> that he who is, is alive. Impulse may be at rest, but when the word 'doing' becomes appropriate, then already there is creativity. (1986, p.39)

Winnicott is not talking just about the physical existence of the body, but the kind of existence in which the individual is sensitive to all that surrounds her, receptive, and ready to shape. This kind of aliveness cannot accommodate doubt, and our creativity can only surface when doubts disappear.

LIMITS

> *The more constraints one imposes, the more one frees one's self of the chains that shackle the spirit.*
>
> Igor Stravinsky

Restrictions bring freedom. Or, as Stephen Nachmanovitch put it, "Structure ignites spontaneity" (1990, p.83). Limits prevent the improviser from wandering around on the surface of ideas, movements, and concepts, and guide her as she searches deeper. Working without constraints often causes the improviser to fall into old habits, such as repeating the same movement patterns. This, in turn, leaves her feeling guilty, bored, unproductive, unsatisfied, and like she is carrying out an action just out of duty. Of course one does not always slip into old habits in an open improvisation with no set limits, but there is a higher risk in this setting, particularly for beginners. In *Landscape of the Now: A Topography of Movement Improvisation*, movement artist, master teacher, and researcher Kent de Spain reports on his interviews with established movement improvisation experts. He indicates that the:

> ...idea of establishing and working within constraints—of space or time or movement vocabulary or anything else—appeared in the interviews again and again in different guises. I have noticed that the most experienced practitioners often choose to work within the tightest constraints. People new to improvisation might find this surprising because it may seem contradictory to the prevalent idea of improvisation as open or free, but such constraints allow

> you to be more aware of what is happening in the moment and, therefore, to more easily see the possibilities for play within that context. Too much freedom can mean too much information upon which to act, like trying to drive a car while making a pizza. (2014, pp.36–37)

This is why learning to give oneself limits is an important asset. Tasks, constraints, and improvisation exercises, while limiting in certain ways, can also open up opportunities and guide us into uncharted territory, delivering the pleasure, satisfaction, and excitement that come from discovery. While one can start an improvisation with some limits already set, integrating new rules over the course of the improvisation can also be helpful. Cansu Kul recounted that in the past she often repeated certain movements she felt comfortable with, and this tendency frustrated her. Now, she says,

> When I find myself stuck in one of these movement habits I try to divert myself from it with another movement. I don't try to go into feelings, ideas, or concepts. I choose a physical limit. It constrains my body in a certain way but at the same time leads me into new grounds where I can grow in a new way. The limit usually inspires a new movement quality. It feels refreshing and I just start shaping it from there on.

It is important to set limits that are just sufficient enough so that the constraints imposed on certain elements of the improvisation empower and enlarge the play range of the improviser without completely immobilizing her. For example, if I set myself the task of crossing the studio while keeping my hands on the floor and my hip off it while trying to physically initiate the movement from my head, it will probably be too much. But carried out in separate exercises, these and similar restrictions over the years have given me new inspirations every time, and helped me experience undiscovered connections between my body parts, nuances of movements, and dynamic ranges.

As I mentioned in Chapter 4, I find it exceptionally productive to prepare myself with intermodal exercises. In my improvisation process I do not think of these exercises as just a part of my *Passage* but integrate them into the movement improvisation. I know improvisers who do not use other disciplines in their process so I cannot say that this is a "*muss sein*," but expanding my improvisation research and process beyond the dance discipline to the entire EXA field has provided me with great benefits. Paolo Knill explains, in *Minstrels of Soul* (Knill *et al.* 2004), that we must not forget we can imagine, speak, move, sound, and act through words, visual images, movement, actions, sound, and rhythm. Each art form is linked to one or multiple sensory modalities during both the expression and the perception stages (see Table 6.1).

Table 6.1. Art forms and their modalities

Art form	Sensory modality traditionally engaged during expression	Sensory modality traditionally engaged during perception
Painting, drawing	Visual, sensorimotor	Visual
Sculpture	Tactile, visual, sensorimotor	Visual; tactile and sensorimotor if permitted by exhibitor
Music	Auditory, visual, sensorimotor	Auditory *(recordings)* Visual *(TV, concerts)* Sensorimotor *(dance)*
Dance	Sensorimotor, visual, auditory	Visual; auditory; sensorimotor when dancing with others
Poetry, prose, literature	Verbal representation of auditory and visual	Auditory *(recital)* Visual *(reading)*
Theater, opera	Auditory, visual, sensorimotor	Auditory, visual

Source: Knill, quoted in Knill et al. (2004, p.44)

Knill argues that, "the conduciveness of modalities for expression, communication and perception always influences one's choice of art form in an expression, even though the influence may be working beneath our awareness" (quoted in Knill *et al.* 2004, p.45). When the need for a certain sensory modality keeps rising to the surface, it is best to integrate this need into the movement improvisation through an exercise. The art form that engages that modality changes the dynamics of the movement and enlarges the playground.

But let us not forget that we are talking about the power of limits. In *The Creative Habit*, choreographer Twyla Tharp talks about a box that she keeps while she is working on an artistic project. It is a box into which she puts everything that inspires her in the making of that project. "The box makes me feel organized," she says, and "that I have my act together even when I don't know where I am going yet" (2003, p.81). The tasks, limits, and exercises that we use in improvisation are like that box. If there is a box, no matter how big or small, we can stow things in it. We can eliminate the things that will not fit in the box, we can see if the things we have put in it so far are enough for us to work with; because there is a frame, there is the box. And as Tharp says: "Before you can think out of the box, you have to start with a box" (2003, p.78).

Limits not only guide us into feeling freer in our medium but also provide us with the opportunity to be transformed with the appearance of the *third* way. In one of our sessions Sarven Çankar built a sculpture from wooden Tegu building blocks that have magnets in them (see Figure 6.2). Later, as he was dancing an improvisation, he unintentionally hit his sculpture with his leg and the structure fell apart. He turned and looked at his transformed piece and screamed the word "water" at it. Afterwards, as we spoke about this, Sarven explained: "It felt as if the sculpture fell apart so that I would see the new shape that it took and scream the word 'water' at it. I don't know where that word came from but it felt as if everything happened so that I would scream that word." He was filled with the startling feeling of the emergence of the *third* way.

Figure 6.2. Sarven Çankar's Tegu magnetic wood block sculpture

Chapter 7

LIMITATIONS OF THIS STUDY AND PROPOSALS FOR FUTURE RESEARCH

> *It is paradoxical, yet true, to say, that the more we know, the more ignorant we become in the absolute sense, for it is only through enlightenment that we become conscious of our limitations.*
>
> *Precisely one of the most gratifying results of intellectual evolution is the continuous opening up of new and greater prospects.*
>
> Nikola Tesla

LONGITUDINAL STUDY

Phenomenology and arts-based research provide a closer look at the meanings that participants attach to improvisation. In this respect, they are potentially more instructive in illuminating this artistic process than a positivist approach, which relies on quantifiable observations that lend themselves to statistical analysis. But because these approaches provide a more natural way of diving into the creative processes of individuals, during the phenomenological research for this book many personal topics related to the Divers' lives—centering around their decisions, concerns, and experiences—began to surface. Since Expressive

Arts (EXA) architecture is designed as a session model for therapy, it was sometimes challenging for me to balance the personal healing characteristic of the process with my research needs. With this in mind, most of the time I ended up extending the length of each session from the anticipated two hours to four. To carry this research even further, I recommend pursuing a longitudinal study that follows these or other Divers over a longer period of time for more sessions.

Another concern that came up, particularly in terms of my interest in the benefits of intermodal exercises, was the reluctance of one of the Divers to explore art forms in which he had little previous training or experience. While he was comfortable with letting-go in movement because of his movement background as a dancer, he questioned every action he took during an exercise with clay modeling, and could not proceed to making a sculpture. Later he explained that he believed in accumulating knowledge before diving into a new medium, and was therefore uncomfortable with pursuing an exercise in an art form for which he had not yet acquired the skills. In a sustained study, this finding and how to address it practically in improvisation would need to be addressed.

Transforming this research into a longitudinal study could also be beneficial in another way. Even though my work with the Divers has convinced me that realizing and/or finding the interplay of letting-go and shaping can be a vital tool for improvisation, particularly when it allows the performer to tap into a multiplicity of opposing ideas, this research, as well as my previous experience teaching performing arts at a university level for eight years, has also taught me that depending on their level of experience, some improvisers may need extended practice before they can fully integrate these concepts and be able to arrive at letting-be. In order to benefit from the perspectives of more advanced improvisers who have extensive experience in letting-be, I included comments from interviews that others and myself conducted with professionals. A longitudinal study would make it possible to further develop and potentially change the perspectives of these and other, future Divers, as they gained more experience.

INTERACTIVE MEDIA

In addition to selecting commonly practiced multi-disciplinary artistic mediums such as sculpture, drawing, writing, and vocalizing, I created interactive environments for my research. One of the designs I utilized was a projection that worked like a magic mirror, showing live video footage of the participant on a wall of the studio. In the projected visual, the movements of the Diver were transformed in real time into a form of light that followed her, enabling the performer to improvise with her transformed video double (see Figure 7.1). Introducing the option of improvising with one's own image brought up many issues for discussion involving, among other questions, the perception of time, the potential insight gained from seeing oneself in a transformed visual image, and the emotional and intellectual reflections and reactions this provokes. While some of the Divers found the integration of these installations inspired them to be more playful, and helped them to let-go, others found seeing a reflection of themselves disturbing. Some explained that they did not want to look at the projection because they did not feel ready to look at themselves. I did not incorporate most of the data from these sessions into my book because I found it to be under-developed, but further research into the effects of integrating interactive media into *the Passage* and *Journey* processes of an improvisation could be productive.

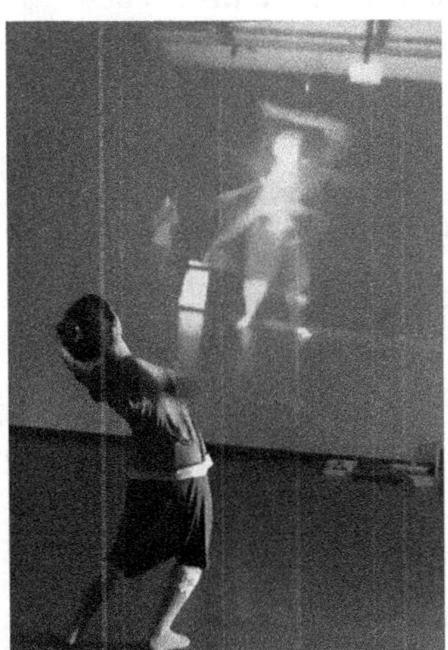

Figure 7.1. Gülce Oral improvising with one of the interactive installations

CONNECTIONS BETWEEN VARIOUS OTHER ARTISTIC MEDIUMS AND MOVEMENT IMPROVISATION

Another topic that came up as I was conducting my research was the relationship of different mediums with movement improvisation. In the one-to-one sessions with the Divers, I used the intermodal exercises both as preparations for and as tools in movement improvisation. As Knill mentions in *Minstrels of Soul* (Knill *et al.* 2004), different artistic mediums offer various strengths for awakening the various forms of an individual's sensitivity. The importance of the connection between other mediums and movement became clearer to me as I realized my inclination to choose intermodal exercises, which resulted in three-dimensional artistic pieces. In my EXA-based work conducted prior to my book research, I was not particularly inclined towards one medium over another. In the sessions with the Divers, I felt inspired to give exercises that used space rather than paper. Even when I would direct them into writing a poem, I ended up giving them various concrete materials so that they could write the poem on their surface and then place them in the space (see Figures 7.2 and 7.3). Preparing the individual for movement improvisation by raising her sensitivity to space is only one of the connections that came up. I believe that many other ideas would flourish if further research is explored into the relationships between various artistic mediums such as drawing, sculpting, singing, installation-making, writing, painting, and movement.

Figures 7.2 and 7.3. Poetry written by Gülce Oral on wooden pieces

CHAPTER 8

CONCLUSIONS

Was he a beast if music could move him so? He felt as if the way to the unknown nourishment he longed for were coming to light.

Franz Kafka

Throughout this book I have demonstrated the critical importance of receptivity in transforming the letting-go and shaping aspects of improvisation into a combined force of letting-be. In Chapter 4, I described some of the essential requirements for heightening the sensitivity of the improviser and preparing her for a productive improvisation session. In Chapter 5, I shared and analyzed the different experiences and processes of the Divers in order to describe in detail the letting-go, shaping, and letting-be states. In Chapter 6, I focused on the "*muss sein*"s that help the improviser create an interplay between her letting-go and shaping forces.

All these chapters rely on the principle that giving permission for an action to shape you *is in itself shaping*. When the improviser empowers her letting-go and shaping forces with this understanding, their relationship transforms itself into an interplay, through being *etken* and *edilgen* interchangeably. With this idea in mind, I have divided my conclusions into three parts: understanding; Expressive Arts (EXA) and improvisation; personal conclusions.

Part I

The Understanding

MULTIPLICITY

The interplay of shaping and letting-go is achieved through an element of receptive attunement in being *etken* and *edilgen*. When there is no receptivity, they remain active and passive without listening and being open to being affected by each other. The receptive interplay of letting-go and shaping lifts the improviser into a state of multiplicity in which different views of and possibilities for approaching the space and developing movement exist together in one person. Psychologist James Hillman describes multiplicity as a "therapeutic tool in order to bring home the realization that 'the ego complex is not the only complex in the psyche'" (Hillman 1989, p.47). Hillman takes it further to explain:

> By actively imagining the psyche into multiple persons, we prevent the ego from identifying with each and every figure in a dream and fantasy, each and every impulse and voice. For the ego is not the whole psyche, only one member of a commune. Therapy works through the paradox of admitting that all figures and feelings of the psyche are wholly 'mine,' while at the same time recognizing that these figures and feelings are free of my control and identity, not 'mine' at all. (1989, p.47)

In improvisation, multiplicity implies the quality of holding together a variety of ideas, feelings, thoughts, and inspirations, even those usually considered oppositional. Therefore, even before the improviser begins, she needs to open herself up to the idea of multiplicity, to the possibility that letting-go and shaping will each provide her with multiple fields and influences with various suggestions to offer. It is the capability of letting this variety find form that makes each improviser unique. The most common problem that surfaces with beginners is that they tend to think of being in the moment as requiring a complete letting-go. They try to clear themselves from the shaping force (an impossible task) without realizing that it is this very shaping that creates their personal style, individual perspective, and uniqueness. In their constant battle of trying to let-go, they become so aware of their fight that it becomes even more impossible to let-go. In one of our sessions, Gökdağ Yalçın described his experience during a Butoh (a form of Japanese dance theater) exercise. The exercise called for him to stand still for 40 minutes, but after 5 minutes he started questioning whether he was going to be able to continue, and after a few more, his discomfort with the idea of just standing there and not doing anything was almost unbearable. He felt as though he had to fight to keep going. Then all of a sudden he had an epiphany and told himself, "Don't define it as a fight. If you define it that way you will lose." How we define challenges has the capacity to change the way we experience them. It is the act of "defining" that holds great potential in general. In my opinion, defining wholeness and letting-be as states that allow one to access multiplicity will also provide new ways of experiencing them. With this understanding, the two heads of the dragon (letting-go and shaping) start to work together and the interplay they create empowers their existence as a whole.

ELASTOPLASTICITY

How we generally visualize, perceive or even define ourselves before, during, and after we live through this state of multiplicity—letting-be—can also change the way we experience it. When letting-go and shaping create a productive interplay, the improviser suddenly has multiple options for inventing movement. Because of the interplay, rather than dividing the two forces in the improvisation, she is able to blend them together and access multiplicity. Some improvisers think of this letting-be (being in the moment) as a state in which they reach a kind of existence they had forgotten, a state they were in before their bodily or conscious existence in this world began. Others evoke having experienced letting-be in their dreams. Thus letting-be can be filled with a sensation of going back to an earlier time and remembering. Sarven Çankar universalizes this sensation:

> Being in the moment is a sumptuous feeling. The studio, the people, and the objects…everything around me I still see. The perception, though, is like seeing the top of an ancient castle. The atmosphere

> around the castle is ancient, as if for centuries people have been going to this special place. This is like a feeling that can never get lost, as if I am remembering it. This is the first time I am thinking about this feeling with words. This ancient feeling fills me when I am in the moment and it is as if I am coming back to experiencing it because I was meant to find this feeling again.

For another Diver, Hasan Canberk Karaçay, letting-be is filled with a sensation of discovery: "It is as if I have entered the dark. A place that I will get to know and I try to let my pupils grow."

During the course of this research, as I have been trying to visualize the individual before, during, and after the state of letting-be (whether she was filled with a sensation of remembering like Sarven or with the excitement of discovery like Canberk), I wondered if plasticity would be an applicable image. Plasticity has been a concept that has been researched and applied to many areas including philosophy, chemistry, and medicine. Neurologist and psychoanalyst Sigmund Freud, as well as philosophers Georg Wilhelm Friedrich Hegel, Georges Canguilhem, and Catherine Malabou, for example, have researched the self as it relates to plasticity in various ways. The term "plastic" has multiple ordinary meanings. While it can refer to material that is "able to be deformed in any direction and to retain its deformed condition permanently without rupture" (like clay, once it hardens into ceramics) it can also refer to one who is "capable of forming" (such as a plastic surgeon) (Barnhart 1973, p.847). In the philosophical sense of the word, Malabou explains:

> Plasticity signifies the general aptitude for development, the power to be molded by one's culture, by education. We speak of the plasticity of the newborn, of the child's plasticity of character. Plasticity, in another context, is characterized by 'suppleness' and flexibility, as in the case of the 'plasticity' of the brain. Yet it also means the ability to evolve and adapt. It is this sense we invoke when we speak of a 'plastic virtue' possessed by animals, plants, and, in general, all living things. (Malabou [1996] 2005, p.8)

Malabou also points out that it is important not to confuse plastic with polymorphous. She explains that while the word "plastic" as an adjective is in clear opposition to fixed, rigid, and ossified, things that are plastic once configured preserve their shape and cannot recover their original form (Malabou [1996] 2005).

Malabou concentrates on three principles of plasticity: to take form, to give form, and explosion of form. As she talks about the plasticity of the human brain, she explains that Alzheimer's and other diseases as well as traumas show how the brain can take form and is plastic because the patients go through a change and reformation rather than a returning to a past stage (which would be the case with elasticity as it relates to reversals to past states). While the brain constantly gives form to our actions and life through its ideas, dreams, and thoughts, the explosion of its form takes place at death. Malabou sees death as a destruction of form, which creates a new form. In her understanding, plasticity "characterizes a regime of systematic self-organization that is based on the ability of an organism to integrate the modifications that it experiences and to modify them in return" ([2005] 2010, p.61).

In the context of EXA, decentering as a method for expanding one's play range offers great possibilities for actualizing plasticity. Decentering exercises transport the individual from the literal realities of her current state to her imaginary possibilities. They propose a break from circular thinking patterns. Arts-based improvisational exercises involving decentering can create new emotional, intellectual, and conceptual perceptions as well as change existing ones.

So if we think of letting-be as a plastic process similar to that described by Malabou—that starts out as malleable but eventually becomes "fixed"—this would mean that the improviser would always stay in the state that letting-be has carried her into. The imagined idea of plasticity would result in letting-be becoming the improviser's everyday essential state as she completes her improvisation and returns to daily life outside of the studio. According to Stephen Levine, "No matter how close the relationship seems between art and life, they will never be identical; and it is in the difference that separates them that the value of art emerges" (2009, p.37). In everyday life, staying constantly in a state of letting-be is not possible. Letting-be is a state in which the letting-go and shaping forces of an improviser exist in an *I–Thou* relationship.

As Buber explains it, "Every *Thou* in the world is by its nature fated to become a thing, or continually to re-enter into the condition of things" (1958, p.17). Therefore both forces are meant to become the *I*s of *I–It*s while they are not in a letting-be state. Apart from her improvisation process the improviser also benefits greatly from the *I–It* states of these forces. For example, a fully concentrated shaping can create miracles as a choreographer enters editing mode. And a highly concentrated letting-go is capable of giving birth to a genius idea that solves a knot of problems with one touch. So there are also benefits of not staying in the achieved form of letting-be.

Finally, I decided to visualize an individual capable of reaching the state of letting-be as an elastoplastic form (a physics term) that shows both elastic and plastic properties. Barnhart describes elastic defined as "having the quality of returning to its original size, shape or position after being stretched, squeezed, bent" (1973, p.352). When elastoplastic forms stretch pass a certain elastic limit, the original form that they go back to (as it stops to stretch) changes. Is improvisation a journey forward to something new, or back to remembering something we had forgotten? I think it can encompass both. (Of course this is not a truth that is proven by research but my attempt to explain the phenomenon.) Bearing the properties of both elasticity and plasticity also supports the understanding of letting-be as a state of multiplicity in which differences and oppositions can exist together.

In improvisation the plastic properties of an elastoplastic individual are realized through letting-go and shaping. Plasticity enables the improviser to discover new grounds or remember old grounds in new ways. She can give them form through shaping, and can find form through letting-go. The fusing of the methods of letting-go and shaping is made possible through their interplay, in the state of letting-be.

Elasticity of the elastoplastic individual is realized when the improviser ends the improvisation process and transforms her sensitivity to internal and external stimuli to an everyday level. At the point of ending the improvisation, elasticity also manifests itself in the shift of the relationship between letting-go and shaping, from one of *I–Thou* to one of *I–It*.

As mentioned above, another property of elastoplastic forms is that as they stretch pass a certain elastic limit, the form that they go back to (as it stops to stretch) changes. So when an improviser experiences the interplay of letting-go and shaping in order to transport her to a state of letting-be, I see this as the elastic limit of an elastoplastic form. If the improviser reaches this state of letting-be, then even when the relation changes and both become the *I*s of the *I–It* for each other, the improviser is transformed. She cannot go back to how she was before this experience (which would have been the case in elasticity). Her experience of letting-be during improvisation flows into her routine life and therefore she is transformed. Eyüp Emre Uçaray experienced this change in the way he took notes. In one of our sessions as he was doing a writing exercise, he explained that he felt as if the paper was taking in what he was writing and therefore there was a deeper relationship between the pen and the paper. He expressed in the next session that until this experience, even though he would always take notes in rehearsals and in his everyday life, because of his messy handwriting he was never able to read them afterwards. But after his experience in the session, even though he was not always feeling the intense connection he felt between the pen and the paper that day, his notes became much neater because the meaning of the physical process of writing changed for him. Another example of how letting-be changes an individual's everyday life was given by Gülce Oral. She expressed that before our sessions she was seeing her shaping force as a voice that had to be hushed. The transformation of this understanding happened through both the improvisational and language-based parts of our sessions. She explained that as she embraced shaping in improvisation, she was able to channel the same understanding to all aspects of her life, and her stress level was lowered.

If letting-go and shaping do not open themselves to each other in order to become receptive, they cannot become *etken* and, in the full sense of the word, *edilgen*. They will just remain active and passive. This relationship will prevent them from creating an interplay and therefore from entering the state of letting-be. The improvisation thus remains under the exclusive control of either shaping or letting-go. When this is the case, the discovery of something new, the emergence of the "third way," becomes impossible. And the lack of the third way disables the individual from reaching the elastic limit. As shown in Figure 8.1, the interchanging *etken* and *edilgen* states of letting-go and shaping trigger a domino effect that results in elastoplasticity.

Receptivity of *etken* and *edilgen*

↓

The interplay of letting-go and shaping (the *I–Thou* relationship)

↓

Being in the moment, the state of letting-be

↓

Emergence of something new, the "third way"

↓

Reaching the elastic limit, elastoplasticity

↓

Transforms the original form, carries the experiences of the improvisation into the daily life of the improviser, and transforms the individual

Figure 8.1. The domino effect

Part II

Expressive Arts and Improvisation

My book research involved applying EXA-based models in an improvisation process. The EXA school of thought, with its focus on multiplicity and its intermodal approach, has provided a highly resourceful session architecture to dive into the phenomenological research of this book. The Divers and I did not just improvise and then talk about it, but also researched the process through experiencing the improvisation, exploring this experience with intermodal artistic methods, and then analyzing it. In the course of this research I realized that an improviser can be supported, inspired, motivated, and highly nurtured from integrating certain approaches and methods of EXA into her working process. What follows are the three main approaches that I have been able to observe and experience the benefits of in the creative process of a performing artist: intermodal approach, decentering, and aesthetic analysis.

INTERMODAL APPROACH

Crystallization is the act of "forming [and] solidifying into crystals," which are "regularly shaped masses with angles and flat surfaces, into which many substances solidify" (Barnhart 1973, p.269). It can also refer to the formation of ideas into definite shapes. In the crystallization theory of EXA, "the metaphor of crystallization is used to explain how in an environment 'saturated' with artistic imagination, a small creative act, seen as a 'seed,' will grow. The growth, following ancient traditions of the arts, reveals the seed's full power with the clarity and order of a crystal" (Knill *et al.* 2005, p.123). Arts-based decentering methods aim to crystallize dreamed or verbalized images into pictures or sculptures, movements into dance, actions into theater, sounds, whistles or moans into music, and poetic scenes into poetry. The theory is built on recognizing the distinctive strengths of individual artistic disciplines and adopting an intermodal approach in order to raise sensitivity and empower different modalities of imagination, such as image, movement, act, word, sound, and rhythm. For the individual who uses improvisation as a tool for creating a performance, the "seeds" of crystallization can be fruitful. They have the potential to grow into concepts and ideas that can transform a creative work or provide an alternative path for the artist when she feels stuck. As dancers we tend to always search for ways of fertilizing the soil for these "seeds" with movement, but sometimes what we need is for our imagination to be triggered by another modality. Practicing intermodal exercises before diving into the improvisation (while going through *the Passage*), during *the Journey* or after *the Journey* has been completed, can enable us to access our imagination through multiple channels and transform both our experience and, potentially, the outcome. In addition to awakening the different sensory mechanisms of the improviser, these exercises can also enhance the improvisation by evoking memories, sensations, sentiments, and ideas that dance alone might not be able to access. Incorporating intermodal exercises at different junctures of the improvisation process also furnishes a wider range of materialized concepts, feelings, and thoughts for the improviser that are created through various modalities of imagination. In the end it is up to the individual to pick and choose, discard, and connect these elements in various forms while composing a piece. Even if she decides to retain them in the finished performance, the act of having discovered them will enrich her movement.

DECENTERING

Philosopher, psychologist, and educational reformer John Dewey asserts that art "enables us to forget ourselves by finding ourselves in the delight of experiencing the world about us in its varied qualities and forms" (1934, p.110). Decentering in an EXA therapy session is the part of the session in which through art-making, play, and/or ritual the client decenters into the imaginary reality. Its main aim is to expand the range of play. In a therapy setting the change agent can choose how close to or removed from the client's concern to design the model of the decentering exercise. In an educational setting, I find theme-far decentering, which makes sure that there is not a direct link between the concern of the client and the theme of the exercise, to be remarkably inspiring for the students. When they start out with their projects, their minds are stuck revolving around the same ideas for their themes. Most of the time their biggest worry is that they will not be able to progress beyond these ideas to find new connections and inspirations. They complain that their play range is limited and confined. Most of the time it is not that they lack the will to discover or the courage to play in unknown territory, but the methods to break out of their insular circle of ideas. This circle is often constricted to the first sets of ideas, movements, and concepts that come to them.

Theme-far decentering that liberates the client from the restricted view of her immediate preoccupations and transfers her to a freer space for play is a helpful method for discovering the spheres that are beyond the artist's first circle of ideas. It provides access to liminality, an in-between stage in which the individual finds herself in an unknown territory dominated by confusion but that also holds promising potential for creating something new. No matter what the purpose of the improvisation is—movement with the goal of creating choreography, warming up, improvisation for its own sake, preparing for an improvisation performance—decentering can become a great tool of creative expansion.

AESTHETIC ANALYSIS

Through its concentration on *poiesis* (art-making and enhancing the capacity to respond and shape the world) (Levine, quoted in Knill *et al.* 2005) EXA promotes the importance of believing in the power of seeing, hearing, tasting, smelling, and touching one's creations—not getting stuck (as most of us do) on thinking that you already know all of these, but stepping away from what you have created and perceiving and evaluating it from a wider perspective.

The aesthetic analysis part of an EXA session follows the phase of decentering into an imaginary reality through art-making. In aesthetic analysis the client describes both the process and the finished work. The change agent intervenes when necessary.

In the aesthetic analysis the client is supposed to stay on the surface by talking about what she actually observes rather than her interpretations of what she sees. Staying on the surface in this way protects both the client and the change agent from attaching superficial meanings to what they see. Lingering on the surface also opens up the potential for seeing new things. Almost every time that I have been involved in an aesthetic analysis (whether as the client or the change agent), I have observed that in the beginning it feels hard to stick to the surface and resist the urge to analyze. We generally feel the need to tie experiences and perceptions to meanings immediately. If we resist this urge to interpret and persist in simply observing, then our field of observation might actually broaden, enabling us to notice new facts or even acquire new ways of looking at our older perceptions. For example, a few years ago I underwent an EXA therapy session as a client. I was seeking perspective and help resolving a concern that I had about teaching. The change agent directed me into writing a poem. As I read the finished work to the change agent, it seemed straightforward. Even though the change agent had instructed me not to look for connections and deeper meanings at the beginning of the aesthetic analysis part, I could clearly see how my poem was connected to the concern I had brought into the session. Only because the change agent kept asking me to stay on the surface was I able to read the words in a different way and clear the channels for the memory of a traumatic moment to rush into my mind. I realized that the poem was not about my concern about teaching, but rather, about a personal concern I had in a relationship. Eventually, going into the details of both my personal and teaching dilemmas helped me realize the deeper problem behind both these issues. Through looking at the surface in detail I was able to find new paths in my words that revealed connections and causes.

Another example in which the aesthetic analysis part of the session completely changed the perspective of the improviser happened in a session with Eyüp Emre Uçaray. As he was improvising (4 meters away from the window), he started looking at the window and was able to vaguely see a reflection of himself. Physically he started playing with the timing of his breath and the voices he created as he took it in and let it out. Later in the aesthetic analysis he explained that he imagined the distance between him and window to be a well. His reflection was down in the well as his physical body was out in the world looking at it. He expressed that as he improvised with his voice, a story started building up for him. His physical body and his reflection were two different voices that belonged to him. When he closed his eyes, the vocal improvisation expressed the feelings and thoughts of the physical body. When he opened his eyes, he was becoming his reflection and the feelings and thoughts of the Emre that was down in the well were being vocalized. As we proceeded with the aesthetic analysis he realized that it was as if he was setting a border and dividing himself up as creative Emre (the one in the well) and regular Emre. There were mixed emotions of jealousy and selfishness that regular Emre was feeling towards the creative one. After analyzing his improvisation in detail he started talking about the limited possibilities of this perspective of dichotomy, and moved forward to thinking about the *third* way.

Applied to material artworks like sculptures, paintings, installations, and literature, aesthetic analysis and observing the surface in detail is easier. With improvisation (if there is not a videotape of the session), aesthetic analysis can be undertaken based on the improviser's description of the process as she recalls it. Of course if the session had a change agent or a witness, their descriptions can also be integrated. I find aesthetic analysis to also be a valuable tool for improvisers who want to develop their movement ideas into choreography. It opens up new ways of seeing and understanding their movements and of finding connections. It provides a second opportunity to access the movement, through memory. In my post-improvisation state, while the most powerful moments and most effective movement phrases certainly linger, if I do not pursue an immediate aesthetic analysis, I do not retain anything else. If I undertake an aesthetic analysis, then I make a conscious effort to remember the improvisation from the beginning to the end. Even if I am undertaking this alone, I make sure that I either explain it out loud or write it down. Of course I do not remember everything even if I implement this process, but some moments of it start re-surfacing. As I hear myself explaining or as I see my written words appear on the page, new connections, reflections, observations, feelings, ideas, and concepts immediately start emerging. Aesthetic analysis is a resourceful tool for the creative process of an artist.

PART III

Personal Conclusions

In the course of planning, researching, and writing this book, I have experienced the "liminality" in almost every aspect of my life. As my confusion and the feeling of powerlessness became more intense, I remembered the words of the Sufi poet Rumi, "The hurt that we embrace becomes joy. Call it to your arms where it can change." As I kept repeating these lines I found myself in the studio looking for a way to transform the darkness of my liminality. I wanted to work on creating a performance piece and asked my colleague, actor Oğuzhan Ayaz, to collaborate with me in this process.

I came to the first rehearsal with a song that I had recently heard and a poem I wrote. I had heard the song in a small concert by the group Nai Dünya, and there was no recording of it yet because it was brand new. The lyrics belonged to the famous Turkish Sufi poet Yunus Emre. I changed the order of some of the lines and the final version that we practiced in the studio was like this:

Poem 1. Adım Adım İleri by Yunus Emre

Adım adım ileri	Forward, step by step
Beş alemden içeri	Through five realms
Oldost ile buluştum	I met with the truest friend
Gördüm bir dağ içinde	I saw him in a mountain
Gözler gibi görmedim	I didn't see it with my eyes
Söz gibi söyleşmedim	I didn't speak like words
Dedim bu kimin ola	I asked to whom this belongs
Sordum bir dağ içinde	I asked in a mountain
Gökler gibi gürledim	I thundered like skies
Yeller gibi inledim	I moaned like winds
Sular gibi çağladım	I gurgled like waters
Aktım bir dağ içinde	I flew in a mountain.

As we practiced the song together and apart, I realized that the song became *the Passage* for this piece. It was our preparation to raise our sensitivities and really feel each other. The final version that we decided on was that we would sit on the floor face-to-face, our knees touching, and sing this song together.

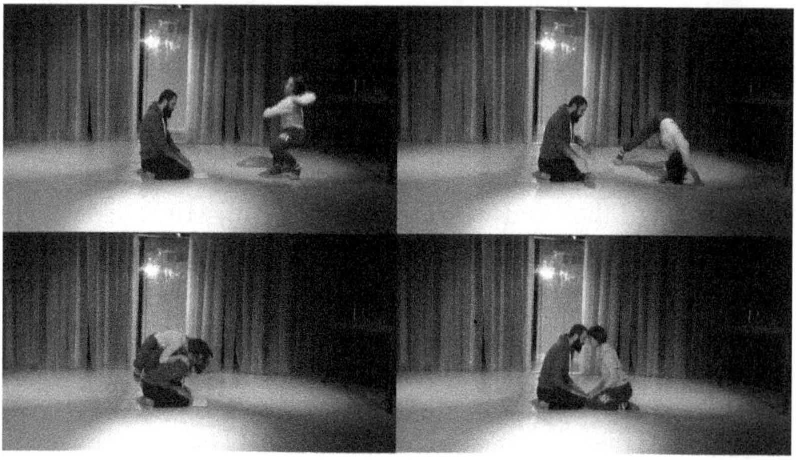

Figure 8.2. Oğuzhan Ayaz and myself in rehearsal

It was more complicated to find the next part of the process. In one of my alone improvisation sessions, I wrote a poem (see Poem 2). The poetic language articulated the meaning of my experiences of shaping and letting-go and enabled me to understand it in a cognitive as well as bodily way. I wanted to incorporate this poem into my work with Oğuzhan. I did not know if we were both going to move, if one of us would read the poem, or if it would be a sound recording. I came to each rehearsal with ideas only to realize that they were disasters. They did not work and I felt stuck. For reasons that were unclear to me, I was resisting my constant need to look at the relationship of letting-go and shaping while two people would symbolize each aspect. The process started to evolve much more smoothly as I incorporated the theme of my book, the interplay of letting-go and shaping, into my process of organizing the rehearsal setting. Before I was trying to shape through preconceived ideas, and it was not working. As I calmed down and enabled my letting-go and shaping forces to create a receptive interplay, I found the form I wanted to explore. Oğuzhan would read the poem and I would dance. He searched through different ways of reading it while I searched through movement. As we kept practicing I realized a reason behind my choice of giving us two separate mediums. I felt that if letting-go and shaping were talking in me, they were speaking different languages. I felt that if I supported them in becoming more receptive to each other, they would easily overcome this difference of the language and would communicate at a deeper level. If they were not receptive, they became more aware of the difference of their languages and got anxious. Because Oğuzhan was searching through reading/acting and I through movement, I was kind of separating our "languages." In our improvisations he felt closer to representing the shaping force and I the letting-go. As we practiced and found ways to sense and play with each other, our mediums merged and some of the experiences I had inspired my decisions as I was writing this book. I saw the edges of the cliffs that doubts create. I was able to return from those cliffs and stroll around, with the overwhelmingly exquisite feeling of surrender. I was freed by the set limits. I realized that raising my sensitivity to both internal and external factors enabled me to discover something new, even in my most habitual movements.

Poem 2. The poem I wrote in one of the improvisation sessions

Zamanın başlangıcından önce	Before the beginning of time,
Her şeyin başlangıcından önce	Before the beginning of everything,
Başlangıçtan önce...	Before there was a beginning…
Dağların, denizlerin, ormanların	A dragon beyond the mountains,
Ötesinde bir ejderha...	oceans and forests…
Yok bu öyle başlamıyor	No it doesn't start this way.
İki kişi	Two people,
Düet	A duet.
Aslında hikaye burada da başlamıyor.	It actually doesn't start this way either.
Onun biriyle dansederken hissettiği	It starts with a dragon that she felt when
Bir ejderhayla başlıyor hikaye	she was dancing with someone else.
Çift başlı bir ejderha	A two-headed dragon.
Dışındakilerden başlayarak hissettiği	That she started feeling through the

Sonra içinde	things outside.
bulduğu/karşılaştığı	Then slowly she found it in her.
Siyah beyaz değil, uzak yakın değil.	Not black and white, not close and far.
Grilerde gezen,	Two heads that travel around the greys
Aynı vücuda sahip çift başlı bir ejderha.	and share a body.
Onun içinde yaşayan.	That live in her.
Biri bırakarak	One has the intention of owning the
anın sahibi olma derdinde	moment through letting-go
Diğeri de şekillendirerek.	And the other through shaping.
An, zaman, vakit.	Instant, time, moment.
Hepsi genişlemiş bekliyor	All expand and wait
Ejderha dediğin şey vahşi	The dragon is wild
Hem tutkuyla tek başına	Each head wants to direct the body alone
yönetmek istiyor bedeni	But also loses power as it defeats the
Hem de güçten düşüyor diğeri yenildikçe	other
Biri geçmişin toplamı	One is the sum of the past
Diğeri şu anın	And the other sum of now.
Çift başlı bir ejderha	A two-headed dragon
Onun içinde yaşayan	That lives in her
Zıttı değiller birbirlerinin,	They are not the opposites of each other,
Farklılar sadece.	They are just different.
An, zaman, vakit.	Instant, time, moment.
Hepsi genişlemiş bekliyor.	All expand and wait.
Bekleyiş zaman alıyor.	Waiting takes time.
Dalmış anın içine	It dives into the moment,
İsterse genişlemesin zaman	Time has no option but to expand.
Bekleyiş içeride arayıp duruyor.	Waiting searches inside.
Biri geçmişin toplamı	One is the sum of the past
Diğeri şu anın	And the other sum of now.

We have not completed this piece or brought it to a level where we could show it as an excerpt, but it has been highly influential and productive for me in order to experience my book process as a dancer and choreographer. All the conclusions of my research are findings that I started integrating into my personal and professional career. The one that I keep telling myself currently is the importance of cleaning oneself from self-judgment, limiting the amount of preconceived ideas, and surrendering to both letting-go and shaping.

THE GRAIL

As I went through the journey of this book, my research, which I believe will continue as long as I live, was enriched by the inspiring experiences, interpretations, thoughts, ideas, visualizations, and artworks of my colleagues, teachers, friends, and the Divers.

As I began my research, the image that kept coming to me was of myself as a two-legged turtle walking down a dirt path. My shell was on my back. The sky was almost but not yet entirely dark, or maybe the sun was about to rise. I was walking with a stick in my hand. I could not see the path because of the obscurity. The forest that surrounded me was colored in all shades of blue—even the ferns, trees, and leaves. As I progressed in my research the image changed. I was still in the blue dark forest, but the peripheries of my path were covered with trays of pastries and fruits. Even though the forest was dark, these trays were illuminated from above, as if by a spotlight whose source was invisible. Today, as I conclude some of my research with this book, I still see myself continuing to follow this path, with trays of pastries and fruits flanking me on both sides. All the different flavors that I have gathered and continue to gather from these trays nurture me. They are the invaluable experiences of others who have been generous enough to share those experiences and the fruits of those experiences with me. And in spite of all the different ways that each one of us has perceived and visualized the state of letting-be, we have had one thing in common: the sparks that we all had in our eyes as we spoke about this inspiring, wondrous state.

When an improviser samples the sensation of letting-be for the first time, she becomes addicted. She yearns to reach that elevated state that pours passion into her, whether it be filled with happiness, anger, sadness, regret, laughter, revenge, or joy. Our two-headed dragon, our forces of shaping and letting-go, have the capability to merge their forces to breathe magic into the moment and into us. This state makes our existence more alive and full of possibilities.

CHAPTER 9

RESPONSES FROM THE DIVERS

In this section I represent the responses I received from some of the Divers after my dissertation was completed.

GÜLCE ORAL

There was a girl.
A curious girl.
Every night,
while all her family was at home drinking tea over trivial conversations,
she snuck out to the garden.
She liked it when it was dark.
When the garden seemed bigger, almost endless.
Some nights,
when she felt more courageous than usual,
she dared to explore the untrodden parts of this garden.
That night was one of those nights.
She felt the power of the moon
revealing the hidden creatures of the night
traces of the darkness.
That night she was silent, careful, alert.
That night, as she thought she reached the confines,
the garden grew bigger.
That night she stole down the new path appearing in front of her

and found a wishing well.
She felt shivers.
Good shivers of a first discovery.
Curious she was,
she wanted to know how deep the well was and what was in it.
She hung down from her chest to see
but it was pitch dark.
She could not tell.
She dropped a piece of rock,
heard the rock dropping against some mud
but she could not tell.
She screamed into it.
She could not tell.
The more she tried different ways to get to know the nature of
this well,
her desire to know grew stronger.
She decided to make her way down the well.
She found some trunks, some branches and sticks;
dropped them in the well, up against its cold stone wall;
hoping to build a pile to land on without hurting herself and
a pile to help her climb back up.

She was careful but not hesitant.
She dangled her legs down,
then her chest,
then her waist, then her hips.
searching with her feet, for the trunks she had placed.
Her arms were getting weaker and weaker.
She had to let go.

She fell.
She fell.
She fell. Down the well.
Just like Alice.
The well did not seem to end.
She felt shivers. Shivers of fear. Her heart started pounding.
Her body was signaling death.
She was panicking.
She was soon to hit the ground and shatter.

She was still falling.
She screamed her lungs out.
She cried her eyes out.
This was the end of life as she knew it.
She was not ever going to hug her mom again.
She was never going to smell her favorite pillow before drifting into dream land. Never going to play with her friends again,
Never to see the moon, never to see the sun.
She was so preoccupied with this wave of fear and regret
that she was no longer aware of her falling.
Then,
in a gap of her terror,
she realized, that she was not falling,
she was rather floating.
She was just floating in empty space.
In this space of her curiosity.

With this new information she opened her eyes wide to see.
It was dark she could not see.
She opened her arms wide to feel.
She felt cold damp walls of stone.
She tried to climb up the walls. It was slippery. She was just hanging in the air.
She weltered there for a while.
Nothing was happening. There was no use. She was stuck in the air.

Then,
She finally gave in,
she calmed down.
She even got comfortable in the well.
Her breath got deeper.
Her senses grew sharper.
Her muscles relaxed.
Then, she felt that she was not alone in this darkness.
She felt the presence of something else.
A kindred spirit.
Something light. Something benevolent.
As she looked with patience, in a new manner,

using her eyes like her ears,
she noticed her faint shadow floating with her.
But there was no light, how can there be a shadow?
She searched for the light source.
Nothing.
She then noticed it was not her shadow.
Oh!
She asked: 'Hey, is there anyone in here?'
No answer.
The shadow was flickering like a candle flame.
As she watched with patience she heard the shadow speaking to her.
Not in words,
not in sound but in its own language.
She heard the shadow speaking deep in her heart.
Like a deeper knowing.
She could only listen.
'Dance' said the shadow. 'Dance your way out.'
She did not understand how dancing could help her out of this strange situation.
She had no other hope.
So she just listened to this invitation.
And she moved. She danced.
Just inhabiting the space.
Feeling pleasure in her joints.
Just settling in the moment.
In her movement.
She felt free.
Free of fear, free of regrets, free of future, free of the well.
She noticed light was pouring in the empty space.
She started seeing the color of darkness.
She looked up
and saw the beautiful stars at night.
She figured she was floating up.
She was wrong.
The walls were gone.
The moment she felt free,
The well was no more.

CANSU KUL

For me, most of our sessions with Beliz were on my inability to set free my thoughts, emotions, and therefore my body. When we were working on these issues, I had been dancing for the past ten years and I had graduated from university. Therefore my awareness of my body and its capabilities was high. This awareness brought me the realization that there could be different reasons for the shallow situation that I kept falling into during improvisation. I realized in the course of our work together that this situation was directly related to my personal life.

In one of the sessions, Beliz asked me to use few different materials including aluminum foil in the movement improvisation. I wanted to bring forth this material especially because the relationship I built with it communicated a lot to me. At the beginning of the improvisation I was clearly aware of the materials, the studio, the music, and Beliz. It was as if my consciousness was looking at myself from an outer eye. But at the end I had an experience that I fully realized after our exercise was finished. My hands and legs were scratched all over in the improvisation. I had not realized it at all while I was dancing. When I saw that some parts of my body were bleeding, I understood that I had cut it with the aluminum foil. When I looked back, none of the movements that I did at those times were from my overly used movement vocabulary. I was not dancing. I was moving and I did not care what it was transforming into. Over the years I had had very few experiences like this one in which I had the feeling of first losing and then finding myself.

Later, our conversations and the written book showed me that my inability of letting-go in improvisation was a problem that I was facing a lot in my daily life. I was unable to let people, circumstances, and incidents flow, and my act of constantly interfering was detaching me from living the moment. Apart from changing the methods and the quality of my improvisations, these sessions affected my personal life directly. Now, whenever I feel like I am being detached from the moment, I think of the exercises we did.

Apart from noticing why my body is inclined to certain movements, the points that detach and the factors that distance me from a concentrated improvisation, these sessions also helped me in finding some answers for my personal life. The soul affects the dance, the dance affects the improvisation, the improvisation affects the unconscious, and I realized again how much each one of these feeds the other.

GÖKDAĞ YALÇIN

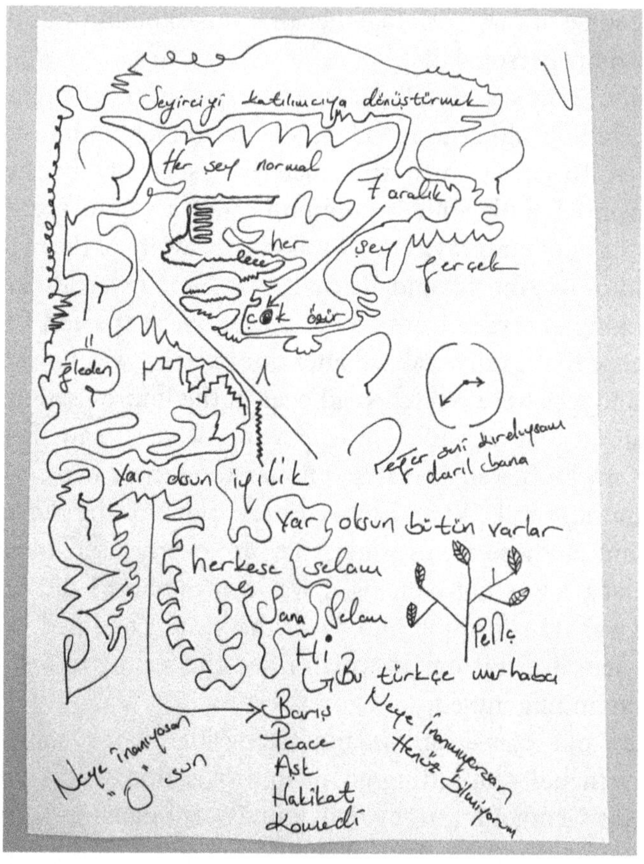

Figure 9.1. Gökdağ Yalçın's aesthetic response

Some moments are beautiful.
Some things that I feel at certain moments are beautiful.
What happened in those moments and I was able to feel that way?
How can I sustain these feelings?

While it seems like some of the rational data that I found as I was searching in order to answer these questions are helping me, in another way they limit these feelings. Some of the rational data imprison the feeling to themselves. They make the feeling dependent on those factors and block the way to find another path to it. In the sessions with Beliz, we worked on breaking free from this imprisonment. We constantly repeated the phrase low skill/high sensitivity. I think it is a great luxury to be in a doctoral dissertation while attending to your feelings in context to it. Because usually it feels like we are supposed to pay attention to things that are outside of us, things that are not directly related to the unique person that we are. For example, one can be interested in an art form for years, like dance. After years, when she comes to a point where she feels that the art form is finding its unique form inside of her, then she wishes that she could have felt this at the beginning. I wish this. What I mean to say is not about changing or not changing the form. It is not even really about the form. But it is about feeling it.

HASAN CANBERK KARAÇAY

> A human being is made up of worries.

This line appears at the beginning of the film *Thou Gild'st the Even* (written and directed by Onur Unlu). Even though it is passed on as if it was quoted from Euripides, there are various rumors about the source of the quote. Without getting into who actually said it, I continue:

> I was worried. While trying to create—while challenged in the act of creating—I just wanted to produce something genuine and in fact, only something that came from me.

I memorized being genuine as my "first principle" in the process of creating—I attribute this choice to my childhood and youth. And now I am trying to be honest. This is one of my priorities. (Even though, when expressed this way, it sounds as if I am an artist who already left behind his youth; I am aware of the fact that I am at the beginning of everything.)

> I was worried, as if the moment of production and the work produced and processed were entities outside of me. I did not notice that I was working on my 'Self.'

On stage—when it comes to theater or dance—the work that I do has no existence outside of my self. Maybe it is true for plastic arts, photography, or painting but in my case it does not work this way. I cannot separate myself from my persona. Even if I am impersonating a character that is completely opposite to mine, there is something related to me, my "Self," about this character; I am impersonating that character. This character comes alive through my voice, my body, my rhythm. This idea comforts me; I remember that I am accountable to myself before any witness sees my work.

When I remembered and read about the time that we worked together, I realized that time has alleviated the burdens I was carrying or changed their form.

Now—of course—I have other worries.

> There is a place for you too
> For you too
> Inside
> In you
> A place
> Definitely exists.
>
> Passing right through all the yous known to you
> Similar to all the you's
> Similar to the ones you touch
> the real touch
> definitely exists—
> A crier
> Comparing them to you
> Calling out to the one far away
> Exists.
>
> Like the longest branch
> Of an old willow tree
> A you
> inside of you

whose beauty is never doubted
who like the willow tree
exists.
Not because I want it
But because I believe it;
It definitely exists.

Before the zeros and ones
An eye amazed by the moon in the sky
Exists inside of you.
An 'I'
Who sees the good
Before wonder,
Who points at the soil first.
I hope,
Exists
Inside of me.

CHAPTER 10

LAST WORDS...

In the course of writing my dissertation a green tea ritual had arisen in the process. I would start writing at night after everyone had gone to sleep, but before I started, I would make myself a green tea and drink it, just sitting at the kitchen table. Me, my tea, the night, and the silence before the words would start dancing.

After the defense of my dissertation, I went on a trip to Japan. I had the enriching opportunity of wandering in the streets of Kyoto and improvising my day. Because of my own green tea ritual I wanted to learn more about the Japanese tea ceremony. I went to a touristy place where one could both attend the ceremony and also learn about how to prepare the tea and other details. This was a few months after my nephew had passed on and I still sometimes found myself lost in endless fields of grief. The teacher at the tea ceremony told us that each day he would choose some calligraphy to hang in the room to designate a theme for the ceremony, a message for his guests. This time, he had chosen the legend of the koi fish. The story went like this: there was a group of golden koi fish swimming up the stream. They gained power by fighting against the current, but as they came up to a waterfall, all but one of them gave up. The one remaining koi fish kept jumping and jumping for years. It seemed impossible for him to jump up to the waterfall, but the fish kept trying, and after a hundred years, it was able to reach the top.

As I left the tea ceremony I wanted to visit the Yasaka Shrine that was close by, but the main entrance of the Shrine was closed for the day. So I started walking aimlessly into Maruyama Park. I just kept walking without realizing that the road had taken me into the Yasaka Shrine through another door. I sat down somewhere and looked at the floor as thoughts moved freely in my mind. As I stood up, I realized that I was sitting right next to a golden panel, and right on the side of it was the embossed story of the koi fish…

My dear reader, I believe that there is a reason when something finds you. This book found you and you found it. This research is for you to let in, shape, personalize, and carry further. I hope that it will encourage you in diving in and then swimming up the waterfalls.

Figure 10.2. My final artistic response to this research.
Photograph taken by Aylin Vartanyan Dilaver

References

American Ballet Theatre (no date) 'Manèges', Ballet Dictionary. Accessed on 4/26/18 at www.abt.org/education/dictionary/index.html

Barnhart, C.L. (1973) 'Plastic.' In *Thorndike Barnhart Student Dictionary* (p.847). Glenview, IL: Scott Foresman and Company.

Biemel, W. and Saner, H. (eds) (2003) *The Heidegger–Jaspers Correspondence (1920–1963).* (Gary E. Aylesworth, Trans.) New York: Humanity Books.

Broadhurst, S. (2007) *Digital Practices: Aesthetic and Neuroesthetic Approaches to Performance and Technology.* New York: Palgrave Macmillan.

Brown, S. (2010) *Play.* New York: G.P. Putnam's Sons.

Buber, M. (1958) *I and Thou (2nd edn).* New York: Charles Scribner's Sons.

Cools, G. (2012) *Body: Language #1. The Mythic Body: Guy Cools with Sidi Larbi Cherkaoui.* London: Sadler's Wells, Arts in Society, Fontys School of Fine and Performing Arts.

Cooney, S. (2016) *Craniosacral Practice.* Available at www.shannoncooney.org/craniosacral-practice/10-craniosacral-practice

Csikszentmihalyi, M. (1990) *Flow: The Psychology of Optimal Experience.* New York: HarperCollins Publishers.

Csikszentmihalyi, M. (1996) *Creativity: Flow and the Psychology of Discovery and Invention.* New York: HarperCollins Publishers.

Dalí, S. and Lorca, F.G. with C. Maurer (ed.) (2004) *Sebastian's Arrows, Letters and Mementos of Salvador Dalí and Federico García Lorca.* Chicago, IL: Swan Isle Press.

de Spain, K. (2014) *Landscape of the Now: A Topography of Movement.* New York: Oxford University Press.

Dewey, J. (1934) *Art as Experience.* New York: Penguin Group.

Fluid Midline (2013) In *Craniosacral Biodynamics.* Available at www.craniosacral-biodynamics.org/glossary.html

Fraleigh, S. (1998) 'A Vulnerable Glance: Seeing Dance Through Phenomenology.' In A. Carter (ed.) *The Routledge Dance Studies Reader* (pp.135–144). London: Routledge.

Gordon, M. (2011) 'Listening as embracing the other: Martin Buber's philosophy of dialogue.' *Educational Theory 61,* 2, 207–219.

Hara, M. (2014) *Aşkın İstilası YOL [Invasion of Love: The Path].* Istanbul: Destek Yayınları.

Herrigel, H. (1953) *Zen in the Art of Archery.* New York: Random House, Inc.

Hillman, J. (1989) *A Blue Fire: Selected Writings by James Hillman.* Introduced and edited by Thomas Moore in collaboration with James Hillman. New York: Harper & Row.

Kafka, F. ([1915] 2003) *The Metamorphosis.* Auckland, New Zealand: The Floating Press.

Knill, P.J., Barba, H.N. and Fuchs, M.N. (2004) *Minstrels of Soul: Intermodal Expressive Therapy.* Toronto, ON: EGS Press.

Knill, P., Levine, E.G. and Levine, S.K. (2005) *Principles and Practice of Expressive Arts Therapy: Towards a Therapeutic Aesthetics.* Philadelphia, PA: Jessica Kingsley Publishers.

Ladinsky, D. (1996) *I Heard God Laughing. Renderings of Hafiz.* Oakfield, CA: Mobius Press.

Leavy, P. (2009) *Method Meets Art.* New York: The Guilford Press.

Levine, S.K. (2009) *Trauma, Tragedy, Therapy. The Arts and the Human Suffering.* London: Jessica Kingsley Publishers.

Levine, S.K. (2013a) 'Expecting the unexpected: Improvisation as a method in art-based research.' *Journal of Applied Arts & Health 4,* 1, 2.

Levine, S.K. (2013b) *Poiesis, Researching Art: The Art of Research (Volume Fifteen).* Toronto, ON: EGS Press.

MacGregor, N. (2010) *A History of the World in 100 Objects.* London: Penguin Books.

Malabou, C. ([1996] 2005) *The Future of Hegel: Plasticity, Temporality and Dialectic.* (L. During, Trans.) New York: Routledge.

Malabou, C. ([2005] 2010) *Plasticity at the Dusk of Writing: Dialectic, Destruction, Deconstruction.* (C. Shread, Trans.) New York and Chicester: Columbia University Press.

Merleau-Ponty, M. (1962) *Phenomenology of Perception.* (C. Smith, Trans.) London: Routledge & Kegan Paul Ltd.

Mungan, M. (1992) *Yaz Geçer [Summer Passes].* Istanbul: Metis Yayınları.

Nachmanovitch, S. (1990) *Free Play: Improvisation in Life and Art.* New York: G.P. Putnam's Sons.

Püsküllüoğlu, A. (1994a) 'Edilgen.' In *Arkadaş Turkish Dictionary.* Ankara: Arkadaş Yayınevi.

Püsküllüoğlu, A. (1994b) 'Etken.' In *Arkadaş Turkish Dictionary.* Ankara: Arkadaş Yayınevi.

Rilke, R. (1984) 'Duino Elegies.' *The Selected Poetry of Rainer Maria Rilke.* (S. Mitchell, Ed. and trans.) New York: Vintage.

Sacks, O. (1985) *The Man Who Mistook His Wife for a Hat.* London: Picador.

Safa, P. (1924) *Bir Akşamdı.* İstanbul: Ötüken Neşriyat.

Stravinsky, I. ([1942] 2003) *Poetics of Music in the Form of Six Lessons.* Translated by Arthur Knodel and Ingolf Dahl. Cambridge, MA: Harvard University Press.

Tesla, N. (1915) *The Wonder World to Be Created by Electricity.* Available at www.tfcbooks.com/tesla/1915-09-09.htm

Tharp, T. with Reiter, M. (2003) *The Creative Habit: Learn It and Use It for Life.* New York: Simon & Schuster Paperbacks.

Tunçer, K. (2007) *Hüsn-ü Aşk'a Dair...* İstanbul: İstanbul State Opera and Ballet House.

Turner, E. (2008) 'Exploring the work of Victor Turner: Liminality and its later implications.' *Suomen Antropologi: Journal of the Finnish Anthropological Society 33,* 4, 26–44.

Turner, V. (1979) *Process, Performance and Pilgrimage: A Study in Comparative Symbology.* New Delhi, India: Naurang Rai Concept Publishing Company.

Turner, V. (1982) *From Ritual to Theater: The Human Seriousness of Play.* New York: PAJ Publications.

van Gennep, A. (1960) *The Rites of Passage.* Chicago, IL: University of Chicago Press.

van Manen, M. (1990) *Researching Lived Experience: Human Science for an Action Sensitive Pedagogy.* New York: State University of New York Press.

Wikipedia (2016a) 'Subliminal stimuli.' Accessed on 4/20/18 at https://en.wikipedia.org/wiki/Subliminal_stimuli

Wikipedia (2016b) 'Craniosacral therapy.' Accessed on 4/20/18 at https://en.wikipedia.org/wiki/Craniosacral_therapy

Winnicott, D.W. (1986) *Home Is Where We Start From: Essays by a Psychoanalyst.* New York: Penguin Books.

Index

Note: page numbers given in italics indicate illustrations